For: _____Felix_____

May the God of peace, equip you with
everything good for doing his will.

Hebrews 13:21

From: _Ms. Hodges & Ms. Gonzalez_

God's Words of Life

*from the Classics
Devotional Bible*

Zondervan*Gifts*
We have a gift for inspiration™

God's Words of Life on

God's Words of Life on
CHALLENGES

These have come so that your faith—of greater worth than gold, which perishes even though refined by fire—may be proved genuine and may result in praise, glory and honor when Jesus Christ is revealed.

1 Peter 1:7

God knows the way that I take; when he has tested me, I will come forth as gold.

Job 23:10

We also rejoice in our sufferings, because we know that suffering produces perseverance; perseverance, character; and character, hope.

Roman 5:3-4

The LORD your God is testing you to find out whether you love him with all your heart and with all your soul.

Deuteronomy 13:3

You know that the testing of your faith develops perseverance. Perseverance must finish its work so that you may be mature and complete, not lacking anything.

James 1:3-4

Strengthen the feeble hands, steady the knees that give way; say to those with fearful hearts, "Be strong, do not fear; your God will come."

Isaiah 35:3-4

God's Words of Life on
CHALLENGES

Blessed is the man who perseveres under trial, because when he has stood the test, he will receive the crown of life that God has promised to those who love him.

James 1:12

Do not be surprised at the painful trial you are suffering, as though something strange were happening to you. But rejoice that you participate in the sufferings of Christ, so that you may be overjoyed when his glory is revealed.

1 Peter 4:12-13

The God of all grace, who called you to his eternal glory in Christ, after you have suffered a little while, will himself restore you and make you strong, firm and steadfast.

1 Peter 5:10

Jesus replied, "Peace I leave with you; my peace I give you. I do not give to you as the world gives. Do not let your hearts be troubled and do not be afraid."

John 14:27

We consider blessed those who have persevered. You have heard of Job's perseverance and have seen what the Lord finally brought about. The Lord is full of compassion and mercy.

James 5:11

God's Words of Life on
CHALLENGES

Jesus answered, "Do not let your hearts be troubled. Trust in God; trust also in me."

John 14:1

Do not be anxious about anything, but in everything, by prayer and petition, with thanksgiving, present your requests to God. And the peace of God, which transcends all understanding, will guard your hearts and your minds in Christ Jesus.

Philippians 4:6-7

Our help is in the name of the LORD, the Maker of heaven and earth.

Psalm 124:8

Blessed is he whose help is the God of Jacob, whose hope is in the LORD his God.

Psalm 146:5

The LORD is good, a refuge in times of trouble. He cares for those who trust in him.

Nahum 1:7

Praise be to the God and Father of our Lord Jesus Christ, the Father of compassion and the God of all comfort, who comforts us in all our troubles, so that we can comfort those in any trouble with the comfort we ourselves have received from God.

2 Corinthians 1:3-4

Devotional Thought on
CHALLENGES

Abundant living is sometimes on account of, but more often, perhaps, in spite of. When circumstances are against us, we must be able to set the sails of our souls and use even adverse winds. The Christian faith does not offer exemption from sorrow and pain and frustration—it offers the power, not merely to bear, but to use these adversities. The secret of using pain and suffering and frustration is in many ways life's greatest secret. When you have learned that, you are unbeatable and unbreakable.

The Christian "can take it," because he can take hold of adversity and use it. Christ bore the cross, for he could use the cross. You cannot bear the cross long—it will break your spirit, unless you can take that cross and make it serve higher purposes. The stoic bears the cross; the Christian makes the cross bear fruit.

Any movement that has learned the secret of making the bitterest tree—the cross—bear the sweet fruit has learned the secret of abundant living.

E. Stanley Jones

God's Words of Life on
CHARACTER

LORD, who may dwell in your sanctuary?
Who may live on your holy hill? He whose
walk is blameless and who does what is
righteous, who speaks the truth from his
heart and has no slander on his tongue, who
does his neighbor no wrong and casts no slur
on his fellowman, who despises a vile man
but honors those who fear the LORD, who
keeps his oath even when it hurts, who lends
his money without usury and does not
accept a bribe against the innocent. He who
does these things will never be shaken.

Psalm 15:1-5

He has showed you, O man, what is good.
And what does the LORD require of you? To
act justly and to love mercy and to walk
humbly with your God.

Micah 6:8

Who may ascend the hill of the LORD? Who
may stand in his holy place? He who has clean
hands and a pure heart, who does not lift up
his soul to an idol or swear by what is false.

Psalm 24:3-4

Be careful that you do not forget the LORD
your God, failing to observe his commands,
his laws and his decrees that I am giving you
this day.

Deuteronomy 8:11

God's Words of Life on
CHARACTER

Blessed is the man who does not walk in the counsel of the wicked or stand in the way of sinners or sit in the seat of mockers. But his delight is in the law of the LORD, and on his law he meditates day and night. He is like a tree planted by streams of water, which yields its fruit in season and whose leaf does not wither. Whatever he does prospers.

Psalm 1:1-3

Do everything without complaining or arguing, so that you may become blameless and pure, children of God without fault in a crooked and depraved generation, in which you shine like stars in the universe.

Philippians 2:14-15

Do not conform any longer to the pattern of this world, but be transformed by the renewing of your mind. Then you will be able to test and approve what God's will is— his good, pleasing and perfect will.

Romans 12:2

For by the grace given me I say to every one of you: Do not think of yourself more highly than you ought, but rather think of yourself with sober judgment, in accordance with the measure of faith God has given you.

Romans 12:3

God's Words of Life on
CHARACTER

Better a poor man whose walk is blameless than a rich man whose ways are perverse.

Proverbs 28:6

Watch your life and doctrine closely. Persevere in them, because if you do, you will save both yourself and your hearers.

1 Timothy 4:16

What does the LORD your God ask of you but to fear the LORD your God, to walk in all his ways, to love him, to serve the LORD your God with all your heart and with all your soul.

Deuteronomy 10:12

Be self-controlled and alert. Your enemy the devil prowls around like a roaring lion looking for someone to devour.

1 Peter 5:8

These are the things you are to do: Speak the truth to each other, and render true and sound judgment in your courts; do not plot evil against your neighbor, and do not love to swear falsely.

Zechariah 8:16-17

Seek good, not evil, that you may live. Then the LORD God Almighty will be with you, just as you say he is.

Amos 5:14

God's Words of Life on
CHARACTER

It is the LORD your God you must follow, and him you must revere. Keep his commands and obey him; serve him and hold fast to him.

Deuteronomy 13:4

Obey your leaders and submit to their authority. They keep watch over you as men who must give an account. Obey them so that their work will be a joy, not a burden.

Hebrews 13:17

This is what the LORD says: "Maintain justice and do what is right, for my salvation is close at hand and my righteousness will soon be revealed."

Isaiah 56:1

Blessed are all who fear the LORD, who walk in his ways. You will eat the fruit of your labor; blessings and prosperity will be yours.

Psalm 128:1-2

The wisdom of the prudent is to give thought to their ways, but the folly of fools is deception.

Proverbs 14:8

Who is wise and understanding among you? Let him show it by his good life, by deeds done in the humility that comes from wisdom.

James 3:13

God's Words of Life on
CHARACTER

He who walks righteously and speaks what is right, who rejects gain from extortion and keeps his hand from accepting bribes, who stops his ears against plots of murder and shuts his eyes against contemplating evil—this is the man who will dwell on the heights, whose refuge will be the mountain fortress. His bread will be supplied, and water will not fail him.

Isaiah 33:15-16

Be very careful, then, how you live—not as unwise but as wise, making the most of every opportunity, because the days are evil. Therefore do not be foolish, but understand what the Lord's will is.

Ephesians 5:15-17

Pursue righteousness, godliness, faith, love, endurance and gentleness. Fight the good fight of the faith. Take hold of the eternal life to which you were called when you made your good confession in the presence of many witnesses.

1 Timothy 6:11-12

Devotional Thought on
CHARACTER

I always like to think of the words of that "great woman" of Shunem. Speaking of the prophet, whom she had observed but whom she did not know well, she said: "I know that this man who often comes our way is a holy man of God" (2 Kings 4:9). It was not what Elisha said or did that conveyed that impression, but what he was. By his merely passing by she could detect something; she could see. What are people sensing about us? We may leave many kinds of impressions: we may leave the impression that we are clever, that we are gifted, that we are this or that or the other. But no, the impression left by Elisha was an impression of God himself.

This matter of our impact upon others turns upon one thing, and that is the working of the Cross in us with regard to the pleasure of the heart of God. It demands that I seek his pleasure, that I seek to satisfy him only, and I do not mind how much it costs me to do so.

Watchman Nee

God's Words of Life on
COMMITMENT

Jesus taught them saying, "Remain in me, and I will remain in you. No branch can bear fruit by itself; it must remain in the vine. Neither can you bear fruit unless you remain in me. I am the vine; you are the branches. If a man remains in me and I in him, he will bear much fruit; apart from me you can do nothing."

John 15:4-5

Forgetting what is behind and straining toward what is ahead, I press on toward the goal to win the prize for which God has called me heavenward in Christ Jesus.

Philippians 3:13-14

Since we are surrounded by such a great cloud of witnesses, let us throw off everything that hinders and the sin that so easily entangles, and let us run with perseverance the race marked out for us.

Hebrews 12:1

I consider everything a loss compared to the surpassing greatness of knowing Christ Jesus my Lord, for whose sake I have lost all things. I consider them rubbish, that I may gain Christ.

Philippians 3:8

God's Words of Life on
COMMITMENT

I consider my life worth nothing to me, if only I may finish the race and complete the task the Lord Jesus has given me—the task of testifying to the gospel of God's grace.

Acts 20:24

Make it your ambition to lead a quiet life, to mind your own business and to work with your hands, just as we told you, so that your daily life may win the respect of outsiders and so that you will not be dependent on anybody.

1 Thessalonians 4:11-12

Jesus replied, "For whoever wants to save his life will lose it, but whoever loses his life for me will find it."

Matthew 16:25

Jesus replied, "The man who loves his life will lose it, while the man who hates his life in this world will keep it for eternal life."

John 12:25

We are hard pressed on every side, but not crushed; perplexed, but not in despair; persecuted, but not abandoned; struck down, but not destroyed. We always carry around in our body the death of Jesus, so that the life of Jesus may also be revealed in our body.

2 Corinthians 4:8-10

God's Words of Life on
COMMITMENT

If we live, we live to the Lord; and if we die, we die to the Lord. So, whether we live or die, we belong to the Lord.

Romans 14:8

No one who puts his hand to the plow and looks back is fit for service in the kingdom of God.

Luke 9:62

I have been crucified with Christ and I no longer live, but Christ lives in me. The life I live in the body, I live by faith in the Son of God, who loved me and gave himself for me.

Galatians 2:20

Do you not know that in a race all the runners run, but only one gets the prize? Run in such a way as to get the prize.

1 Corinthians 9:24

Whatever you do, work at it with all your heart, as working for the Lord, not for men, since you know that you will receive an inheritance from the Lord as a reward. It is the Lord Christ you are serving.

Colossians 3:23-24

Devotional Thought on
COMMITMENT

The pressure of hard places makes us value life. Every time our life is given back to us from such a trial, it is like a new beginning, and we learn better how much it is worth, and make more of it for God and man. The pressure helps us to understand the trials of others, and fits us to help and sympathize with them.

There is a shallow, superficial nature, that gets hold of a theory or a promise lightly and talks very glibly about the distrust of those who shrink from every trial; but the man or woman who has suffered much never does this, but is very tender and gentle, and knows what suffering really means.

Trials and hard places are needed to press us forward, even as the furnace fires in the hold of that mighty ship give force that moves the piston, drives the engine, and propels that great vessel across the sea in the face of the winds and waves.

A. B. Simpson

God's Words of Life on
COMPASSION

Be kind and compassionate to one another, forgiving each other, just as in Christ God forgave you.

Ephesians 4:32

Even in darkness light dawns for the upright, for the gracious and compassionate and righteous man.

Psalm 112:4

Love your enemies, do good to them, and lend to them without expecting to get anything back. Then your reward will be great, and you will be sons of the Most High, because he is kind to the ungrateful and wicked.

Luke 6:35

Be devoted to one another in brotherly love. Honor one another above yourselves.

Romans 12:10

Who is a God like you, who pardons sin and forgives the transgression of the remnant of his inheritance? You do not stay angry forever but delight to show mercy. You will again have compassion on us; you will tread our sins underfoot and hurl all our iniquities into the depths of the sea.

Micah 7:18-19

God's Words of Life on
COMPASSION

As God's chosen people, holy and dearly loved, clothe yourselves with compassion, kindness, humility, gentleness and patience. Bear with each other and forgive whatever grievances you may have against one another. Forgive as the Lord forgave you.

Colossians 3:12-13

You, O LORD, are a compassionate and gracious God, slow to anger, abounding in love and faithfulness.

Psalm 86:15

The Lord is full of compassion and mercy.

James 5:11

He who despises his neighbor sins, but blessed is he who is kind to the needy.

Proverbs 14:21

Administer true justice; show mercy and compassion to one another. Do not oppress the widow or the fatherless, the alien or the poor. In your hearts do not think evil of each other.

Zechariah 7:9-10

Carry each other's burdens, and in this way you will fulfill the law of Christ.

Galatians 6:2

God's Words of Life on
COMPASSION

All of you, live in harmony with one another; be sympathetic, love as brothers, be compassionate and humble. Do not repay evil with evil or insult with insult, but with blessing, because to this you were called so that you may inherit a blessing.

1 Peter 3:8-9

In everything, do to others what you would have them do to you, for this sums up the Law and the Prophets.

Matthew 7:12

Have mercy on me, O God, according to your unfailing love; according to your great compassion blot out my transgressions.

Psalm 51:1

The LORD your God will restore your fortunes and have compassion on you.

Deuteronomy 30:3

The LORD will judge his people and have compassion on his servants when he sees their strength is gone.

Deuteronomy 32:36

As a father has compassion on his children, so the LORD has compassion on those who fear him.

Psalm 103:13

Devotional Thought on
COMPASSION

The combination of great power and great restraint is well-known in civilized life and in the laws of nature. The fire that warms the room when properly regulated, will, if abused, reduce the proudest palaces to ashes. The river, which softens and refreshes the landscape, if allowed to escape its banks, can devastate the most fruitful fields.

In pointing out the terribleness of God, I do not appeal to fear ... We do not say, "Be good, or God will crush you." That is not virtue, that is not liberty—it is vice put on its good behavior. It is iniquity with a sword suspended over its head.

The great truth to be learned is that all the terribleness of God is the good man's security. When the good man sees God wasting the mountains and the hills, and drying up the rivers, he does not say, "I must worship him or he will destroy me." He says, "The beneficent side of that power is all mine. Because of that power I am safe. The very lightning is my guardian, and in the whirlwind I hear a pledge of benediction."

Joseph Parker

God's Words of Life on
CONSCIENCE & MORALS

I will maintain my righteousness and never let go of it; my conscience will not reproach me as long as I live.

Job 27:6

Test me, O LORD, and try me, examine my heart and my mind; for your love is ever before me, and I walk continually in your truth.

Psalm 26:2-3

God holds victory in store for the upright, he is a shield to those whose walk is blameless, for he guards the course of the just and protects the way of his faithful ones. Then you will understand what is right and just and fair—every good path.

Proverbs 2:7-9

I put on righteousness as my clothing; justice was my robe and my turban.

Job 29:14

The integrity of the upright guides them, but the unfaithful are destroyed by their duplicity.

Proverbs 11:3

As long as I have life within me, the breath of God in my nostrils, my lips will not speak wickedness, and my tongue will utter no deceit.

Job 27:3-4

God's Words of Life on
CONSCIENCE & MORALS

I strive always to keep my conscience clear before God and man.

Acts 24:16

Let us draw near to God with a sincere heart in full assurance of faith, having our hearts sprinkled to cleanse us from a guilty conscience and having our bodies washed with pure water.

Hebrews 10:22

My hands have been free of violence and my prayer is pure.

Job 16:17

In your hearts set apart Christ as Lord. Always be prepared to give an answer to everyone who asks you to give the reason for the hope that you have. But do this with gentleness and respect, keeping a clear conscience, so that those who speak maliciously against your good behavior in Christ may be ashamed of their slander.

1 Peter 3:15-16

LORD, who may dwell in your sanctuary? Who may live on your holy hill? He whose walk is blameless and who does what is righteous, who speaks the truth from his heart.

Psalm 15:1-2

God's Words of Life on
CONSCIENCE & MORALS

Though you probe my heart and examine me at night, though you test me, you will find nothing; I have resolved that my mouth will not sin.

Psalm 17:3

For I have kept the ways of the LORD; I have not done evil by turning from my God. All his laws are before me; I have not turned away from his decrees.

Psalm 18:21-22

Let love and faithfulness never leave you; bind them around your neck, write them on the tablet of your heart. Then you will win favor and a good name in the sight of God and man.

Proverbs 3:3-4

The man of integrity walks securely, but he who takes crooked paths will be found out.

Proverbs 10:9

Better a poor man whose walk is blameless than a fool whose lips are perverse.

Proverbs 19:1

It is necessary to submit to the authorities, not only because of possible punishment but also because of conscience.

Romans 13:5

God's Words of Life on
CONSCIENCE & MORALS

He who walks righteously and speaks what is right, who rejects gain from extortion and keeps his hand from accepting bribes, who stops his ears against plots of murder and shuts his eyes against contemplating evil— this is the man who will dwell on the heights, whose refuge will be the mountain fortress. His bread will be supplied, and water will not fail him.

Isaiah 33:15-16

True instruction was in his mouth and nothing false was found on his lips. He walked with me in peace and uprightness, and turned many from sin.

Malachi 2:6

Whoever can be trusted with very little can also be trusted with much, and whoever is dishonest with very little will also be dishonest with much.

Luke 16:10

He who loves a pure heart and whose speech is gracious will have the king for his friend.

Proverbs 22:11

Blessed is the man who does not condemn himself by what he approves.

Romans 14:22

God's Words of Life on
CONSCIENCE & MORALS

One man considers one day more sacred than another; another man considers every day alike. Each one should be fully convinced in his own mind.

Romans 14:5

We have renounced secret and shameful ways; we do not use deception, nor do we distort the word of God. On the contrary, by setting forth the truth plainly we commend ourselves to every man's conscience in the sight of God.

2 Corinthians 4:2

The LORD detests lying lips, but he delights in men who are truthful.

Proverbs 12:22

I will set before my eyes no vile thing. The deeds of faithless men I hate; they will not cling to me. Men of perverse heart shall be far from me; I will have nothing to do with evil.

Psalm 101:3–4

Devotional Thought on
CONSCIENCE & MORALS

Most of us never use our spiritual sense. God has given us a nose to smell with, eyes to see with, hands to feel with, a tongue to taste with. We are made in three parts–body, soul, and spirit. The soul has senses equivalent to those of the body, and the spirit behind that has a third set of senses that an unregenerate man has not commenced to use. But if you are a spiritual man you will use these spiritual senses to discriminate the thoughts as they come to your heart. "By reason of use" you will have your senses exercised to discern both good and evil.

If you live in the midst of bad people, bad books, and bad things, you lose your power of detecting bad thoughts when they come teeming about you like microbes. But if every day you spend an hour on God's mountains or upon the broad sea of the Bible, and get some of God's accurate senses into you, you will be able to detect things which are wrong that other people, even Christians, pass without seeing as wrong.

F. B. Meyer

God's Words of Life on
COURAGE

Do not fear, for I am with you; do not be dismayed, for I am your God. I will strengthen you and help you; I will uphold you with my righteous right hand.

Isaiah 41:10

Dear friends, do not be surprised at the painful trial you are suffering, as though something strange were happening to you. But rejoice that you participate in the sufferings of Christ, so that you may be overjoyed when his glory is revealed.

1 Peter 4:12-13

In all these things we are more than conquerors through him who loved us. For I am convinced that neither death nor life, neither angels nor demons, neither the present nor the future, nor any powers, neither height nor depth, nor anything else in all creation, will be able to separate us from the love of God that is in Christ Jesus our Lord.

Romans 8:37-39

Be strong and take heart, all you who hope in the LORD.

Psalm 31:24

Be strong in the Lord and in his mighty power.

Ephesians 6:10

God's Words of Life on
COURAGE

He gives strength to the weary and increases the power of the weak. Even youths grow tired and weary, and young men stumble and fall; but those who hope in the LORD will renew their strength. They will soar on wings like eagles; they will run and not grow weary, they will walk and not be faint.

Isaiah 40:29-31

Do not be anxious about anything, but in everything, by prayer and petition, with thanksgiving, present your requests to God. And the peace of God, which transcends all understanding, will guard your hearts and your minds in Christ Jesus.

Philippians 4:6-7

Be on your guard; stand firm in the faith; be men of courage; be strong.

1 Corinthians 16:13

Have I not commanded you? Be strong and courageous. Do not be terrified; do not be discouraged, for the LORD your God will be with you wherever you go.

Joshua 1:9

Fear not, for I have redeemed you; I have summoned you by name; you are mine.

Isaiah 43:1

God's Words of Life on
COURAGE

The LORD is my light and my salvation—
whom shall I fear? The LORD is the stronghold of my life—of whom shall I be afraid?

Psalm 27:1

Be strong and courageous. Do not be afraid
or terrified because of them, for the LORD
your God goes with you; he will never leave
you nor forsake you.

Deuteronomy 31:6

When you pass through the waters, I will be
with you; and when you pass through the
rivers, they will not sweep over you. When
you walk through the fire, you will not be
burned; the flames will not set you ablaze.
For I am the LORD, your God, the Holy One
of Israel, your Savior.

Isaiah 43:2-3

Fear of man will prove to be a snare, but
whoever trusts in the LORD is kept safe.

Proverbs 29:25

For God did not give us a spirit of timidity, but
a spirit of power, of love and of self-discipline.

2 Timothy 1:7

Devotional Thought on
COURAGE

A man was obliged to descend into a deep well by sliding down a rope which was to be of ample length. But to his dismay he came to the end before his feet had touched the bottom. He had not the strength to climb up again. To let go and drop seemed to him but to be dashed to pieces in the depths below. He held on until his strength was utterly exhausted, and then dropped, as he thought, to his death. He fell—just three inches—and found himself safe on the rock bottom. Are you afraid to take this step? Does it seem too sudden, too much like a leap in the dark? If ever you are to enter this glorious land, flowing with milk and honey, you must step into the brimming waters, for there is no other path; and to do it now may save you months and even years of disappointment and grief. Hear the word of the Lord—

"Have I not commanded thee? Be strong and of a good courage; be not afraid, neither be thou dismayed: for the Lord thy God is with thee, whithersoever thou goest" (Joshua 1:9, KJV).

Hannah Whitall Smith

God's Words of Life on
ENCOURAGEMENT

As iron sharpens iron, so one man sharpens another.

Proverbs 27:17

Words from a wise man's mouth are gracious, but a fool is consumed by his own lips.

Ecclesiastes 10:12

A man finds joy in giving an apt reply—and how good is a timely word!

Proverbs 15:23

Pleasant words are a honeycomb, sweet to the soul and healing to the bones.

Proverbs 16:24

My mouth would encourage you; comfort from my lips would bring you relief.

Job 16:5

The mouth of the righteous man utters wisdom, and his tongue speaks what is just.

Psalm 37:30

Praise be to the God and Father of our Lord Jesus Christ! In his great mercy he has given us new birth into a living hope through the resurrection of Jesus Christ from the dead, and into an inheritance that can never perish, spoil or fade.

1 Peter 1:3-4

God's Words of Life on
ENCOURAGEMENT

An anxious heart weighs a man down, but a kind word cheers him up.

Proverbs 12:25

He who began a good work in you will carry it on to completion until the day of Christ Jesus.

Philippians 1:6

A cheerful heart is good medicine, but a crushed spirit dries up the bones.

Proverbs 17:22

Every good and perfect gift is from above, coming down from the Father of the heavenly lights, who does not change like shifting shadows.

James 1:17

For the LORD God is a sun and shield; the LORD bestows favor and honor; no good thing does he withhold from those whose walk is blameless.

Psalm 84:11

May our Lord Jesus Christ himself and God our Father, who loved us and by his grace gave us eternal encouragement and good hope, encourage your hearts and strengthen you in every good deed and word.

2 Thessalonians 2:16-17

God's Words of Life on
ENCOURAGEMENT

Do you not know? Have you not heard? The
LORD is the everlasting God, the Creator of
the ends of the earth. He will not grow tired
or weary, and his understanding no one can
fathom. He gives strength to the weary and
increases the power of the weak. Even youths
grow tired and weary, and young men
stumble and fall; but those who hope in the
LORD will renew their strength. They will soar
on wings like eagles; they will run and not
grow weary, they will walk and not be faint.

Isaiah 40:28-31

Encourage one another daily, as long as it is
called Today, so that none of you may be
hardened by sin's deceitfulness.

Hebrews 3:13

Let us not give up meeting together, as some
are in the habit of doing, but let us encourage
one another—and all the more as you see the
Day approaching.

Hebrews 10:25

If you have any encouragement from being
united with Christ, if any comfort from his
love, if any fellowship with the Spirit, if any
tenderness and compassion, then make my
joy complete by being like-minded, having the
same love, being one in spirit and purpose.

Philippians 2:1-2

God's Words of Life on
ENCOURAGEMENT

Everything that was written in the past was written to teach us, so that through endurance and the encouragement of the Scriptures we might have hope. May the God who gives endurance and encouragement give you a spirit of unity among yourselves as you follow Christ Jesus, so that with one heart and mouth you may glorify the God and Father of our Lord Jesus Christ.

Romans 15:4-6

Blessed are those who have learned to acclaim you, who walk in the light of your presence, O LORD. They rejoice in your name all day long; they exult in your righteousness. For you are their glory and strength, and by your favor you exalt our horn.

Psalm 89:15-17

Praise be to the God and Father of our Lord Jesus Christ, the Father of compassion and the God of all comfort, who comforts us in all our troubles, so that we can comfort those in any trouble with the comfort we ourselves have received from God.

2 Corinthians 1:3-4

We will be with the Lord forever. Therefore encourage each other with these words.

1 Thessalonians 4:17–18

God's Words of Life on
ENCOURAGEMENT

You know that we dealt with each of you as a father deals with his own children, encouraging, comforting and urging you to live lives worthy of God, who calls you into his kingdom and glory.

1 Thessalonians 2:11–12

Who shall separate us from the love of Christ? Shall trouble or hardship or persecution or famine or nakedness or danger or sword? No, in all these things we are more than conquerors through him who loved us. For I am convinced that neither death nor life, neither angels nor demons, neither the present nor the future, nor any powers, neither height nor depth, nor anything else in all creation, will be able to separate us from the love of God that is in Christ Jesus our Lord.

Romans 8:35, 37-39

Encourage one another and build each other up, just as in fact you are doing.

1 Thessalonians 5:11

Dear friends, now we are children of God, and what we will be has not yet been made known. But we know that when he appears, we shall be like him, for we shall see him as he is.

1 John 3:2

Devotional Thought on
ENCOURAGEMENT

The wells of the Lord are found where most I need them. The Lord of the way knows the pilgrim life, and the wells have been unsealed just where the soul is prone to become dry and faint. At the foot of the hill Difficulty was found a spring!

Sometimes I am foolish, and in my need I assume that the well is far away. I knew a farmer who for a generation had carried every pail of water from a distant well to meet the needs of his homestead. One day he sunk a shaft by his own house door, and to his great joy he found that the water was waiting at his own gate! My soul, thy well is near, even here! Go not in search of him! Thy pilgrimage is ended, the waters are at thy feet!

But I must "draw the water out of the wells of salvation." The hand of faith must lift the gracious gift to the parched lips, and so refresh the panting soul. "I will take the cup of salvation." Stretch out thy "lame hand of faith," and take the holy, hallowed energy offered by the Lord.

J. H. Jowett

God's Words of Life on
ETERNAL LIFE

Jesus replied, "I tell you the truth, whoever hears my word and believes him who sent me has eternal life and will not be condemned; he has crossed over from death to life."

John 5:24

Jesus answered, "Whoever drinks the water I give him will never thirst. Indeed, the water I give him will become in him a spring of water welling up to eternal life."

John 4:14

Surely goodness and love will follow me all the days of my life, and I will dwell in the house of the LORD forever.

Psalm 23:6

If you confess with your mouth, "Jesus is Lord," and believe in your heart that God raised him from the dead, you will be saved.

Romans 10:9

Jesus said to her, "I am the resurrection and the life. He who believes in me will live, even though he dies; and whoever lives and believes in me will never die."

John 11:25-26

Jesus said, "I tell you the truth, he who believes has everlasting life."

John 6:47

God's Words of Life on
ETERNAL LIFE

Jesus replied, "My sheep listen to my voice; I know them, and they follow me. I give them eternal life, and they shall never perish; no one can snatch them out of my hand."

John 10:27-28

Jesus answered, "Everyone who has left houses or brothers or sisters or father or mother or children or fields for my sake will receive a hundred times as much and will inherit eternal life. But many who are first will be last, and many who are last will be first."

Matthew 19:29-30

For God so loved the world that he gave his one and only Son, that whoever believes in him shall not perish but have eternal life.

John 3:16

God will redeem my life from the grave; he will surely take me to himself.

Psalm 49:15

"The thief comes only to steal and kill and destroy; I have come that they may have life, and have it to the full," Jesus replied.

John 10:10

The man who loves his life will lose it, while the man who hates his life in this world will keep it for eternal life.

John 12:25

God's Words of Life on
ETERNAL LIFE

Now that you have been set free from sin and have become slaves to God, the benefit you reap leads to holiness, and the result is eternal life. For the wages of sin is death, but the gift of God is eternal life in Christ Jesus our Lord.

Romans 6:22-23

Fight the good fight of the faith. Take hold of the eternal life to which you were called when you made your good confession in the presence of many witnesses.

1 Timothy 6:12

This is the testimony: God has given us eternal life, and this life is in his Son. He who has the Son has life; he who does not have the Son of God does not have life.

1 John 5:11-12

Whoever believes in the Son has eternal life, but whoever rejects the Son will not see life, for God's wrath remains on him.

John 3:36

Keep yourselves in God's love as you wait for the mercy of our Lord Jesus Christ to bring you to eternal life.

Jude 1:21

Devotional Thought on
ETERNAL LIFE

It is a question with some whether or not we shall know each other in heaven. Indeed, we shall not know each other after the flesh, not by stature, voice, color, complexion, visage, or outward shape. If we had so known Christ, we should know him no more by parts and gifts of learning, nor titles of honor or worldly dignity; nor any other terms; but by the image of Christ and spiritual relation and former faithfulness in improving our talents, beyond doubt, we shall know and be known.

Nor is it only our old acquaintance, but all the saints of all the ages, whose faces in the flesh we never saw, whom we shall there both know and comfortably enjoy … I think, Christian, this will be a more honorable assembly than ever you beheld and a more happy society than you were ever in before …

What a day will it be when we shall join with them in praises to our Lord in and for that kingdom! So then I conclude, this is one singular excellency of the rest of heaven, that we are "fellow citizens with the saints, and of the household of God" (Ephesians 2;19, KJV).

Richard Baxter

God's Words of Life on
FAITH

Surely this is our God; we trusted in him, and he saved us. This is the LORD, we trusted in him; let us rejoice and be glad in his salvation.

Isaiah 25:9

Jesus replied, "I tell you the truth, whoever hears my word and believes him who sent me has eternal life and will not be condemned; he has crossed over from death to life."

John 5:24

Faith is being sure of what we hope for and certain of what we do not see.

Hebrews 11:1

Faith comes from hearing the message, and the message is heard through the word of Christ.

Romans 10:17

Jesus taught them saying, "I tell you the truth, if you have faith as small as a mustard seed, you can say to this mountain, 'Move from here to there' and it will move. Nothing will be impossible for you."

Matthew 17:20

"Because you have seen me, you have believed; blessed are those who have not seen and yet have believed," Jesus answered.

John 20:29

God's Words of Life on
FAITH

We live by faith, not by sight.

2 Corinthians 5:7

For in the gospel a righteousness from God is revealed, a righteousness that is by faith from first to last, just as it is written: "The righteous will live by faith."

Romans 1:17

Without faith it is impossible to please God, because anyone who comes to him must believe that he exists and that he rewards those who earnestly seek him.

Hebrews 11:6

Everything is possible for him who believes.

Mark 9:23

Let us fix our eyes on Jesus, the author and perfecter of our faith, who for the joy set before him endured the cross, scorning its shame, and sat down at the right hand of the throne of God.

Hebrews 12:2

Though you have not seen him, you love him; and even though you do not see him now, you believe in him and are filled with an inexpressible and glorious joy, for you are receiving the goal of your faith, the salvation of your souls.

1 Peter 1:8-9

God's Words of Life on
FAITH

"Have faith in God," Jesus answered. "I tell you the truth, if anyone says to this mountain, 'Go, throw yourself into the sea,' and does not doubt in his heart but believes that what he says will happen, it will be done for him. Therefore I tell you, whatever you ask for in prayer, believe that you have received it, and it will be yours."

Mark 11:22-24

The only thing that counts is faith expressing itself through love.

Galatians 5:6

Let us draw near to God with a sincere heart in full assurance of faith, having our hearts sprinkled to cleanse us from a guilty conscience and having our bodies washed with pure water.

Hebrews 10:22

Do not throw away your confidence; it will be richly rewarded.

Hebrews 10:35

We fix our eyes not on what is seen, but on what is unseen. For what is seen is temporary, but what is unseen is eternal.

2 Corinthians 4:18

Let us hold unswervingly to the hope we profess, for God who promised is faithful.

Hebrews 10:23

Devotional Thought on
FAITH

If faith ... is a sure persuasion of the truth of God which can neither lie nor deceive us and be neither vain nor false, those who have conceived this certainty surely expect likewise that God will accomplish his promises which, according to their conviction, cannot but be true. So that, in sum, hope is nothing else than the expectation of the things that faith has believed to be truly promised by God. Thus faith believes God to be truthful: Hope expects that he will show his veracity at the opportune time. Faith believes God to be our Father: Hope expects that he will always act as such toward us. Faith believes eternal life to be given to us: Hope expects that it shall at some time be revealed. Faith is the foundation on which hope rests: Hope nourishes and maintains faith. For, just as no one can expect and hope anything from God, except he who will have first believed his promises, so, on the other hand, it is necessary that our feeble faith (lest it grow weary and fail) be sustained and kept by patient hope and expectation.

John Calvin

God's Words of Life on
FAITHFULNESS

My eyes will be on the faithful in the land, that they may dwell with me; he whose walk is blameless will minister to me. No one who practices deceit will dwell in my house; no one who speaks falsely will stand in my presence.

Psalm 101:6-7

Well done, good and faithful servant! You have been faithful with a few things; I will put you in charge of many things. Come and share your master's happiness!

Matthew 25:21

A faithful man will be richly blessed, but one eager to get rich will not go unpunished.

Proverbs 28:20

The Lord is faithful, and he will strengthen and protect you from the evil one.

2 Thessalonians 3:3

If we are faithless, God will remain faithful, for he cannot disown himself.

2 Timothy 2:13

I [the Lord] am with you and will watch over you wherever you go, and I will bring you back to this land. I will not leave you until I have done what I have promised you.

Genesis 28:15

God's Words of Life on
FAITHFULNESS

Being confident of this, that he who began a good work in you will carry it on to completion until the day of Christ Jesus.

Philippians 1:6

The one who calls you is faithful and he [God] will do it.

1 Thessalonians 5:24

Your love, O LORD, reaches to the heavens, your faithfulness to the skies.

Psalm 36:5

God, who has called you into fellowship with his Son Jesus Christ our Lord, is faithful.

1 Corinthians 1:9

No temptation has seized you except what is common to man. And God is faithful; he will not let you be tempted beyond what you can bear. But when you are tempted, he will also provide a way out so that you can stand up under it.

1 Corinthians 10:13

O Lord, I will bow down toward your holy temple and will praise your name for your love and your faithfulness, for you have exalted above all things your name and your word.

Psalm 138:2

God's Words of Life on
FAITHFULNESS

The LORD rewards every man for his right-eousness and faithfulness.

1 Samuel 26:23

I will sing of the LORD's great love forever; with my mouth I will make your faithfulness known through all generations. I will declare that your love stands firm forever, that you established your faithfulness in heaven itself.

Psalm 89:1-2

Righteousness and justice are the foundation of your throne, O Lord; love and faithfulness go before you.

Psalm 89:14

God will cover you with his feathers, and under his wings you will find refuge; his faithfulness will be your shield and rampart.

Psalm 91:4

For the LORD is good and his love endures forever; his faithfulness continues through all generations.

Psalm 100:5

Because of the LORD's great love we are not consumed, for his compassions never fail. They are new every morning; great is your faithfulness.

Lamentations 3:22-23

God's Words of Life on
FAITHFULNESS

Not to us, O LORD, but to your name be the glory, because of your love and faithfulness.

Psalm 115:1

Let love and faithfulness never leave you; bind them around your neck, write them on the tablet of your heart. Then you will win favor and a good name in the sight of God and man.

Proverbs 3:3-4

The fruit of the Spirit is love, joy, peace, patience, kindness, goodness, faithfulness, gentleness and self-control. Against such things there is no law.

Galatians 5:22-23

He is the Rock, his works are perfect, and all his ways are just. A faithful God who does no wrong, upright and just is he.

Deuteronomy 32:4

All the ways of the LORD are loving and faithful for those who keep the demands of his covenant.

Psalm 25:10

Know therefore that the LORD your God is God; he is the faithful God, keeping his covenant of love to a thousand generations of those who love him and keep his commands.

Deuteronomy 7:9

God's Words of Life on
FAITHFULNESS

Love the LORD, all his saints! The LORD
preserves the faithful, but the proud he pays
back in full. Be strong and take heart, all you
who hope in the LORD.

Psalm 31:23-24

The word of the LORD is right and true; he is
faithful in all he does.

Psalm 33:4

The LORD loves the just and will not forsake
his faithful ones. They will be protected
forever.

Psalm 37:28

Let those who love the LORD hate evil, for he
guards the lives of his faithful ones and
delivers them from the hand of the wicked.

Psalm 97:10

The LORD is faithful to all his promises and
loving toward all he has made.

Psalm 145:13

Be joyful in hope, patient in affliction,
faithful in prayer.

Romans 12:12

Let us hold unswervingly to the hope we
profess, for God who promised is faithful.

Hebrews 10:23

Devotional Thought on
FAITHFULNESS

Want of trust is at the root of almost all our sins and all our weaknesses. How shall we escape it but by looking to him and observing his faithfulness? The man who holds God's faithfulness will not be foolhardy or reckless, but he will be ready for every emergency. Abraham held God's faithfulness and offered up Isaac, "accounting that God was able to raise him … from the dead" (Hebrews 11:19, KJV). Moses held God's faithfulness and led the millions of Israel into the howling wilderness. "And what shall I more say? For the time would fail me to tell" of those who, holding God's faithfulness, had faith and by it "subdued kingdoms, wrought righteousness, obtained promises … out of weakness were made strong, waxed valiant in fight, turned to flight the armies of the aliens" (11:33-34, KJV). Satan, too, has his creed: Doubt God's faithfulness. "Hath God said? Are you not mistaken as to his commands?" How constantly, and alas, how successfully are such arguments used to prevent wholehearted trust in God! All God's giants have been weak men, who did great things for God because they reckoned on his being with them.

James Hudson Taylor

53

God's Words of Life on
FORGIVENESS

As far as the east is from the west, so far has he removed our transgressions from us.

Psalm 103:12

When you stand praying, if you hold anything against anyone, forgive him, so that your Father in heaven may forgive you your sins.

Mark 11:25

"I will cleanse them from all the sin they have committed against me and will forgive all their sins of rebellion against me," says the LORD.

Jeremiah 33:8

Bear with each other and forgive whatever grievances you may have against one another. Forgive as the Lord forgave you.

Colossians 3:13

Come now, let us reason together, though your sins are like scarlet, they shall be as white as snow; though they are red as crimson, they shall be like wool.

Isaiah 1:18

"I am he who blots out your transgressions, for my own sake, and remembers your sins no more," says the LORD.

Isaiah 43:25

God's Words of Life on
FORGIVENESS

Blessed is he whose transgressions are forgiven, whose sins are covered. Blessed is the man whose sin the LORD does not count against him and in whose spirit is no deceit.

Psalm 32:1-2

Jesus replied, "I tell you the truth, all the sins and blasphemies of men will be forgiven them."

Mark 3:28

You are forgiving and good, O LORD, abounding in love to all who call to you.

Psalm 86:5

If my people, who are called by my name, will humble themselves and pray and seek my face and turn from their wicked ways, then will I hear from heaven and will forgive their sin and will heal their land.

2 Chronicles 7:14

If we walk in the light, as he is in the light, we have fellowship with one another, and the blood of Jesus, his Son, purifies us from all sin. If we claim to be without sin, we deceive ourselves and the truth is not in us. If we confess our sins, he is faithful and just and will forgive us our sins and purify us from all unrighteousness.

1 John 1:7-9

God's Words of Life on
FORGIVENESS

Peter came to Jesus and asked, "Lord, how many times shall I forgive my brother when he sins against me? Up to seven times?" Jesus answered, "I tell you, not seven times, but seventy-seven times."

Matthew 18:21-22

In Jesus we have redemption through his blood, the forgiveness of sins, in accordance with the riches of God's grace that he lavished on us with all wisdom and understanding.

Ephesians 1:7-8

God has rescued us from the dominion of darkness and brought us into the kingdom of the Son he loves, in whom we have redemption, the forgiveness of sins.

Colossians 1:13-14

The LORD our God is merciful and forgiving, even though we have rebelled against him.

Daniel 9:9

Repent and be baptized, every one of you, in the name of Jesus Christ for the forgiveness of your sins. And you will receive the gift of the Holy Spirit. The promise is for you and your children and for all who are far off—for all whom the Lord our God will call.

Acts 2:38-39

God's Words of Life on
FORGIVENESS

"Their sins and lawless acts I will remember no more," says the Lord.

Hebrews 10:17-18

The LORD is slow to anger, abounding in love and forgiving sin and rebellion.

Numbers 14:18

Praise the LORD, O my soul, and forget not all his benefits—who forgives all your sins and heals all your diseases.

Psalm 103:2-3

Praise be to the Lord, the God of Israel, because he has come and has redeemed his people.

Luke 1:68

He who conceals his sins does not prosper, but whoever confesses and renounces them finds mercy.

Proverbs 28:13

For the sake of your name, O LORD, forgive my iniquity, though it is great.

Psalm 25:11

Be kind and compassionate to one another, forgiving each other, just as in Christ God forgave you.

Ephesians 4:32

God's Words of Life on
FORGIVENESS

Jesus said, "If you forgive men when they sin against you, your heavenly Father will also forgive you. But if you do not forgive men their sins, your Father will not forgive your sins."

Matthew 6:14-15

When we were overwhelmed by sins, you, O Lord, forgave our transgressions.

Psalm 65:3

O LORD, you forgave the iniquity of your people and covered all their sins.

Psalm 85:2

Forgive all our sins and receive us graciously, O LORD, that we may offer the fruit of our lips.

Hosea 14:2

Jesus said, "Do not judge, and you will not be judged. Do not condemn, and you will not be condemned. Forgive, and you will be forgiven."

Luke 6:37

Devotional Thought on
FORGIVENESS

There was a boy who was kidnapped in London. Long months and years passed and the mother had prayed and prayed. All her efforts had failed, and they had given up all hope, all except the mother.

One day a boy was sent into the neighboring house to sweep the chimney, and by some mistake he got down through the wrong chimney. When he came down he came in by the sitting room chimney. His memory began at once to travel back through the years that had passed. He thought that things looked strangely familiar.

As he stood there, covered with rags and soot, his mother came into the room. Did she wait until she had sent him to be washed before she rushed and took him in her arms? No, indeed; it was her own boy. She took him to her arms, all black and sooty, hugged him to her bosom, and shed tears of joy on his head.

You have wandered very far from him, and there may not be a sound spot on you; but if you will just come to God he will forgive and receive you.

Dwight L. Moody   59

God's Words of Life on
FRIENDSHIP

A friend loves at all times, and a brother is born for adversity.

Proverbs 17:17

My intercessor is my friend as my eyes pour out tears to God.

Job 16:20

A man of many companions may come to ruin, but there is a friend who sticks closer than a brother.

Proverbs 18:24

Two are better than one, because they have a good return for their work: If one falls down, his friend can help him up.

Ecclesiastes 4:9-10

Do not make friends with a hot-tempered man, do not associate with one easily angered, or you may learn his ways and get yourself ensnared.

Proverbs 22:24-25

Wounds from a friend can be trusted.

Proverbs 27:6

Perfume and incense bring joy to the heart, and the pleasantness of one's friend springs from his earnest counsel.

Proverbs 27:9

God's Words of Life on
FRIENDSHIP

He who loves a pure heart and whose speech is gracious will have the king for his friend.

Proverbs 22:11

Jesus said, "You are my friends if you do what I command. I no longer call you servants, because a servant does not know his master's business. Instead, I have called you friends, for everything that I learned from my Father I have made known to you."

John 15:14-15

A despairing man should have the devotion of his friends.

Job 6:14

The body is a unit, though it is made up of many parts; and though all its parts are many, they form one body. So it is with Christ.

1 Corinthians 12:12

A gossip betrays a confidence, but a trustworthy man keeps a secret.

Proverbs 11:13

We proclaim to you what we have seen and heard, so that you also may have fellowship with us. And our fellowship is with the Father and with his Son, Jesus Christ.

1 John 1:3

God's Words of Life on
FRIENDSHIP

How good and pleasant it is when brothers live together in unity!

Psalm 133:1

Rejoice with those who rejoice; mourn with those who mourn. Live in harmony with one another. Do not be proud, but be willing to associate with people of low position. Do not be conceited.

Romans 12:15-16

If we walk in the light, as God is in the light, we have fellowship with one another.

1 John 1:7

Jesus said, "Greater love has no one than this, that he lay down his life for his friends. You are my friends if you do what I command."

John 15:13-14

Where you go I will go, and where you stay I will stay. Your people will be my people and your God my God. Where you die I will die, and there I will be buried. May the LORD deal with me, be it ever so severely, if anything but death separates you and me.

Ruth 1:16–17

Devotional Thought on
FRIENDSHIP

A blessed thing it is for any man or woman to have a friend: one human soul whom we can trust utterly; who knows the best and the worst of us, and who loves us, in spite of our faults: who will speak the honest truth to us, while the world flatters us to our faces, and laughs at us behind our backs; who will give us counsel and reproof in the day of prosperity and self conceit; but who again will comfort and encourage us in the day of difficulty and sorrow, when the world leaves us alone to fight our own battles as we can.

If we have had the good fortune to win such a friend, let us do anything rather than lose him. We must give and forgive; live and let live. If our friends have faults we must bear with them. We must hope all things, endure all things rather than lose that most precious of all earthly possessions—a trusty friend. And a friend once won, need never be lost, if we will only be trusty and true ourselves.

Charles Kingsley

God's Words of Life on
GIVING

A generous man will prosper; he who refreshes others will himself be refreshed.

Proverbs 11:25

Jesus taught them saying, "I was hungry and you gave me something to eat, I was thirsty and you gave me something to drink, I was a stranger and you invited me in, I needed clothes and you clothed me, I was sick and you looked after me, I was in prison and you came to visit me."

Matthew 25:35-36

Good will come to him who is generous and lends freely, who conducts his affairs with justice.

Psalm 112:5

He who is kind to the poor lends to the LORD, and he will reward him for what he has done.

Proverbs 19:17

Freely you have received, freely give.

Matthew 10:8

Give generously to him and do so without a grudging heart; then because of this the LORD your God will bless you in all your work and in everything you put your hand to.

Deuteronomy 15:10

God's Words of Life on
GIVING

Remember this: Whoever sows sparingly will also reap sparingly, and whoever sows generously will also reap generously. Each man should give what he has decided in his heart to give, not reluctantly or under compulsion, for God loves a cheerful giver.

2 Corinthians 9:6-7

Do not forget to do good and to share with others, for with such sacrifices God is pleased.

Hebrews 13:16

The wicked borrow and do not repay, but the righteous give generously; those the LORD blesses will inherit the land, but those he curses will be cut off.

Psalm 37:21-22

Blessed is he who is kind to the needy.

Proverbs 14:21

The righteous give without sparing.

Proverbs 21:26

When you give to the needy, do not let your left hand know what your right hand is doing, so that your giving may be in secret. Then your Father, who sees what is done in secret, will reward you.

Matthew 6:3-4

God's Words of Life on
GIVING

Share with God's people who are in need.
Practice hospitality.

Romans 12:13

Give to the one who asks you, and do not
turn away from the one who wants to borrow
from you.

Matthew 5:42

Jesus replied, "Come to me, all you who are
weary and burdened, and I will give you rest.
Take my yoke upon you and learn from me,
for I am gentle and humble in heart, and you
will find rest for your souls. For my yoke is
easy and my burden is light."

Matthew 11:28-30

"My Father will give you whatever you ask
in my name. Until now you have not asked
for anything in my name. Ask and you will
receive, and your joy will be complete," Jesus
replied.

John 16:23-24

Give everyone what you owe him: If you owe
taxes, pay taxes; if revenue, then revenue; if
respect, then respect; if honor, then honor.

Romans 13:7-8

Devotional Thought on
GIVING

Worship is giving God the best that he has given you. Take time to meditate before God and offer the blessing back to him in a deliberate act of worship. If you hoard it for yourself, it will turn into spiritual dry rot, as the manna did when it was hoarded (see Exodus 16:20). God will never allow you to keep a spiritual blessing completely for yourself. It must be given back to him so that he can make it a blessing to others.

The lasting value of our public service for God is measured by the depth of the intimacy of our private times of fellowship and oneness with him. Rushing in and out of worship is wrong every time—there is always plenty of time to worship God. Days set apart for quiet can be a trap, detracting from the need to have daily quiet time with God. That is why we must "pitch our tents" where we will always have quiet times with him, however noisy our times with the world may be.

Oswald Chambers

God's Words of Life on
GRACE

Since we have been justified through faith,
we have peace with God through our Lord
Jesus Christ, through whom we have gained
access by faith into this grace in which we
now stand. And we rejoice in the hope of the
glory of God.

Romans 5:1-2

I always thank God for you because of his
grace given you in Christ Jesus. For in him
you have been enriched in every way—in all
your speaking and in all your knowledge.

1 Corinthians 1:4-5

For it is by grace you have been saved,
through faith— and this not from yourselves, it is the gift of God— not by works,
so that no one can boast.

Ephesians 2:8-9

Do not be ashamed to testify about our Lord
who has saved us and called us to a holy
life— not because of anything we have done
but because of his own purpose and grace.
This grace was given us in Christ Jesus
before the beginning of time, but it has now
been revealed through the appearing of our
Savior, Christ Jesus, who has destroyed death
and has brought life and immortality to light
through the gospel.

2 Timothy 1:8-10

God's Words of Life on
GRACE

Each one should use whatever gift he has received to serve others, faithfully administering God's grace in its various forms.

1 Peter 4:10

From the fullness of God's grace we have all received one blessing after another.

John 1:16

I consider my life worth nothing to me, if only I may finish the race and complete the task the Lord Jesus has given me— the task of testifying to the gospel of God's grace.

Acts 20:24

For sin shall not be your master, because you are not under law, but under grace.

Romans 6:14

My grace is sufficient for you, for my power is made perfect in weakness. Therefore I will boast all the more gladly about my weaknesses, so that Christ's power may rest on me.

2 Corinthians 12:9

Let your conversation be always full of grace, seasoned with salt, so that you may know how to answer everyone.

Colossians 4:6

God's Words of Life on
GRACE

Let us then approach the throne of grace with confidence, so that we may receive mercy and find grace to help us in our time of need.

Hebrews 4:16

Because of his great love for us, God, who is rich in mercy, made us alive with Christ even when we were dead in transgressions—it is by grace you have been saved.

Ephesians 2:4-5

The salvation of the righteous comes from the LORD; he is their stronghold in time of trouble. The LORD helps them and delivers them; he delivers them from the wicked and saves them, because they take refuge in him.

Psalm 37:39-40

You gave me life and showed me kindness, O LORD, and in your providence watched over my spirit.

Job 10:12

Every good and perfect gift is from above, coming down from the Father of the heavenly lights, who does not change like shifting shadows.

James 1:17

Devotional Thought on
GRACE

You probably know the legend of the rider who crossed the frozen Lake of Constance by night unknowingly. When he reached the opposite shore and was told whence he came, he broke down, horrified. This is the human situation when the sky opens and the earth is bright, when we may hear: By grace you have been saved! We are like that terrified rider. When we hear this we involuntarily look back asking ourselves: Where have I been? Over an abyss, in mortal danger! What did I do? The most foolish thing I ever attempted! What happened? I was doomed and miraculously escaped and now I am safe! You ask: "Do we really live in such danger?" Yes, we live on the brink of death. But we have been saved. Look at Jesus Christ on the cross, accused, sentenced, and punished instead of us! Do you know for whose sake he is hanging there? For our sake—because of our sin! He nails our life to the cross. From this darkness he has saved us. He who is not shattered after hearing this news may not yet have grasped the word of God: By grace you have been saved.

Karl Barth

God's Words of Life on
GRIEF & DEATH

Even though I walk through the valley of the shadow of death, I will fear no evil, for you, O LORD, are with me; your rod and your staff, they comfort me.

Psalm 23:4

Precious in the sight of the LORD is the death of his saints.

Psalm 116:15

Now the dwelling of God is with men, and he will live with them. They will be his people, and God himself will be with them and be their God. He will wipe every tear from their eyes. There will be no more death or mourning or crying or pain, for the old order of things has passed away.

Revelation 21:3-4

You guide me with your counsel, and afterward you will take me into glory. Whom have I in heaven but you? And earth has nothing I desire besides you. My flesh and my heart may fail, but God is the strength of my heart and my portion forever.

Psalm 73:24-26

Blessed are those who mourn, for they will be comforted.

Matthew 5:4

God's Words of Life on
GRIEF & DEATH

None of us lives to himself alone and none of us dies to himself alone. If we live, we live to the Lord; and if we die, we die to the Lord. So, whether we live or die, we belong to the Lord.

Romans 14:7-8

We know that if the earthly tent we live in is destroyed, we have a building from God, an eternal house in heaven, not built by human hands.

2 Corinthians 5:1

For to me, to live is Christ and to die is gain.

Philippians 1:21

He died for us so that, whether we are awake or asleep, we may live together with him.

1 Thessalonians 5:10

The eyes of the LORD are on those who fear him, on those whose hope is in his unfailing love, to deliver them from death and keep them alive in famine.

Psalm 33:18-19

Our God is a God who saves; from the Sovereign LORD comes escape from death.

Psalm 68:20

God's Words of Life on
GRIEF & DEATH

If Christ is in you, your body is dead because of sin, yet your spirit is alive because of righteousness. And if the Spirit of him who raised Jesus from the dead is living in you, he who raised Christ from the dead will also give life to your mortal bodies through his Spirit, who lives in you.

Romans 8:10-11

We are confident, I say, and would prefer to be away from the body and at home with the Lord.

2 Corinthians 5:8

Even in death the righteous have a refuge.

Proverbs 14:32

Those who walk uprightly enter into peace; they find rest as they lie in death.

Isaiah 57:2

For I am convinced that neither death nor life, neither angels nor demons, neither the present nor the future, nor any powers, neither height nor depth, nor anything else in all creation, will be able to separate us from the love of God that is in Christ Jesus our Lord.

Romans 8:38-39

Devotional Thought on
GRIEF & DEATH

Some desire to live that they may see more of that glorious work of God for his church. So Moses prayed that he might not die in the wilderness, but go over Jordan, and see the good land, and that goodly mountain and Lebanon, the seat of the church and of the worship of God; which God thought to deny him. This denial of Moses' request, made on the highest consideration possible, is instructive unto all in the like case. Others rise no higher than their own private interests in their persons, their families, their relations, and goods. They would see these things in a better or more settled condition before they die, and then they shall be most willing to do so. But it is the love of life that lies at the bottom of all these desires in men. No man can die cheerfully or comfortably who lives not in a constant resignation of the time and season of his death unto the will of God. Our times are in his hand and his will in all things must be complied withal. Without this resolution, without this resignation, no man can enjoy the least solid peace in this world.

John Owen

God's Words of Life on
GUIDANCE

In your unfailing love, O LORD, you will lead the people you have redeemed. In your strength you will guide them to your holy dwelling.

Exodus 15:13

Lead me, O LORD, in your righteousness— make straight your way before me.

Psalm 5:8

The LORD makes me lie down in green pastures, he leads me beside quiet waters, he restores my soul. He guides me in paths of righteousness for his name's sake.

Psalm 23:2-3

Show me your ways, O LORD, teach me your paths; guide me in your truth and teach me, for you are God my Savior, and my hope is in you all day long.

Psalm 25:4-5

For this God is our God for ever and ever; he will be our guide even to the end.

Psalm 48:14

Good and upright is the LORD; therefore he instructs sinners in his ways. He guides the humble in what is right and teaches them his way.

Psalm 25:8-9

God's Words of Life on
GUIDANCE

Let the morning bring me word of your unfailing love, O LORD, for I have put my trust in you. Show me the way I should go, for to you I lift up my soul.

Psalm 143:8

Teach me to do your will, for you are my God; may your good Spirit lead me on level ground.

Psalm 143:10

Test me, O LORD, and try me, examine my heart and my mind; for your love is ever before me, and I walk continually in your truth.

Psalm 26:2-3

O LORD, since you are my rock and my fortress, for the sake of your name lead and guide me.

Psalm 31:3

O LORD, if you are pleased with me, teach me your ways so I may know you and continue to find favor with you.

Exodus 33:13

Surely you desire truth in the inner parts; you, O God, teach me wisdom in the inmost place.

Psalm 51:6

God's Words of Life on
GUIDANCE

Teach me your way, O LORD, and I will walk in your truth; give me an undivided heart, that I may fear your name.

Psalm 86:11

Restore to me the joy of your salvation, O LORD, and grant me a willing spirit, to sustain me.

Psalm 51:12

May the Lord direct your hearts into God's love and Christ's perseverance.

2 Thessalonians 3:5

The LORD will guide you always; he will satisfy your needs and will strengthen your frame.

Isaiah 58:11

For God, who said, "Let light shine out of darkness," made his light shine in our hearts to give us the light of the knowledge of the glory of God in the face of Christ.

2 Corinthians 4:6

Devotional Thought on
GUIDANCE

We know, our Father, that at this desperate hour in world affairs, we need thee. We need thy strength, thy guidance, thy wisdom. There are problems far greater than any wisdom of man can solve. What shall our leaders do in such an hour?

May thy wisdom and thy power come upon those whom have been entrusted leadership. May the responsibility lie heavily on their hearts, until they are ready to acknowledge their helplessness and turn to thee. Give to them the honesty, the courage, and the moral integrity to confess that they don't know what to do. Only then can they lead us as a nation beyond human wisdom to thee, who alone hast the answer.

Lead us to this high adventure. Remind us that a "mighty fortress is our God"—not a hiding place where we can escape for an easy life, but rather an arsenal of courage and strength the mightiest of all, who will march beside us into the battle for righteousness and world brotherhood.

Peter Marshall

God's Words of Life on
HOLINESS

Now that you have been set free from sin and have become slaves to God, the benefit you reap leads to holiness, and the result is eternal life.

Romans 6:22

Make every effort to live in peace with all men and to be holy; without holiness no one will see the Lord.

Hebrews 12:14

Let us purify ourselves from everything that contaminates body and spirit, perfecting holiness out of reverence for God.

2 Corinthians 7:1

Not that I have already obtained all this, or have already been made perfect, but I press on to take hold of that for which Christ Jesus took hold of me.

Philippians 3:12

May he strengthen your hearts so that you will be blameless and holy in the presence of our God and Father when our Lord Jesus comes with all his holy ones.

1 Thessalonians 3:13

God did not call us to be impure, but to live a holy life.

1 Thessalonians 4:7

God's Words of Life on
HOLINESS

May the God of peace, who through the blood of the eternal covenant brought back from the dead our Lord Jesus, that great Shepherd of the sheep, equip you with everything good for doing his will, and may he work in us what is pleasing to him, through Jesus Christ, to whom be glory for ever and ever.

Hebrews 13:20-21

Your hearts must be fully committed to the LORD our God, to live by his decrees and obey his commands.

1 Kings 8:61

He who pursues righteousness and love finds life, prosperity and honor.

Proverbs 21:21

Be perfect, therefore, as your heavenly Father is perfect.

Matthew 5:48

Jesus said, "If you want to be perfect, go, sell your possessions and give to the poor, and you will have treasure in heaven. Then come, follow me."

Matthew 19:21

Blessed are those who hunger and thirst for righteousness, for they will be filled.

Matthew 5:6

God's Words of Life on
HOLINESS

Seek first God's kingdom and his righteousness, and all these things will be given to you as well.

Matthew 6:33

Pursue righteousness, godliness, faith, love, endurance and gentleness.

1 Timothy 6:11

Consecrate yourselves and be holy, because I am the LORD your God. Keep my decrees and follow them. I am the LORD, who makes you holy.

Leviticus 20:7-8

All the ways of the LORD are loving and faithful for those who keep the demands of his covenant.

Psalm 25:10

Hate what is evil; cling to what is good.

Romans 12:9

You were taught, with regard to your former way of life, to put off your old self, which is being corrupted by its deceitful desires; to be made new in the attitude of your minds; and to put on the new self, created to be like God in true righteousness and holiness.

Ephesians 4:22-24

Devotional Thought on
HOLINESS

I can never sanctify to God that with which I long to satisfy myself. If I am going to satisfy myself with the blessings of God, they will corrupt me; I have to sacrifice them, pour them out, do with them what any commonsense man would say is an absurd waste. Take it in the case of friendship, or of blessing, or of spiritual experiences; as soon as I long to hold any of these for myself I cannot sanctify them to the Lord.

How am I to pour out spiritual gifts, or natural friendship, or love? How can I give them to the Lord? In one way only—in the determination of my mind, and that takes about two seconds. If I hold spiritual blessings or friendship for myself they will corrupt me, no matter how beautiful they are. I have to pour them out before the Lord, give them to him in my mind, though it looks as if I am wasting them; even as when David poured the water out on the sand, to be instantly sucked up.

Oswald Chambers

God's Words of Life on
HONESTY

Have a clear conscience and desire to live honorably in every way.

Hebrews 13:18

Obey your earthly masters in everything; and do it, not only when their eye is on you and to win their favor, but with sincerity of heart and reverence for the Lord. Whatever you do, work at it with all your heart, as working for the Lord, not for men.

Colossians 3:22–23

Whatever is true, whatever is noble, whatever is right, whatever is pure, whatever is lovely, whatever is admirable—if anything is excellent or praiseworthy—think about such things.

Philippians 4:8

Live such good lives among the pagans that, though they accuse you of doing wrong, they may see your good deeds and glorify God on the day he visits us.

1 Peter 2:12

Give the enemy no opportunity for slander.

1 Timothy 5:14

Jesus taught them saying, "In everything, do to others what you would have them do to you, for this sums up the Law and the Prophets."

Matthew 7:12

God's Words of Life on
HONESTY

In everything set an example by doing what is good. In your teaching show integrity, seriousness and soundness of speech that cannot be condemned, so that those who oppose you may be ashamed because they have nothing bad to say about us.

Titus 2:7–8

The grace of God that brings salvation has appeared to all men. It teaches us to say "No" to ungodliness and worldly passions, and to live self-controlled, upright and godly lives in this present age.

Titus 2:11–12

Jesus said, "Do not murder, do not commit adultery, do not steal, do not give false testimony, do not defraud, honor your father and mother."

Mark 10:19

The LORD detests lying lips, but he delights in men who are truthful.

Proverbs 12:22

Keep the way of the LORD by doing what is right and just.

Genesis 18:19

Blessed is the man who does not condemn himself by what he approves.

Romans 14:22

God's Words of Life on
HONESTY

He who walks righteously and speaks what is right, who rejects gain from extortion and keeps his hand from accepting bribes, who stops his ears against plots of murder and shuts his eyes against contemplating evil— this is the man who will dwell on the heights, whose refuge will be the mountain fortress.

Isaiah 33:15–16

He who has clean hands and a pure heart, who does not lift up his soul to an idol or swear by what is false. He will receive blessing from the LORD and vindication from God his Savior.

Psalm 24:4–5

Jesus replied, "Whoever can be trusted with very little can also be trusted with much, and whoever is dishonest with very little will also be dishonest with much."

Luke 16:10

To do what is right and just is more acceptable to the LORD than sacrifice.

Proverbs 21:3

The man of integrity walks securely, but he who takes crooked paths will be found out.

Proverbs 10:9

Devotional Thought on
HONESTY

There is some danger of falling into a soft Christianity, under the plea of a lofty and ethereal theology. Christianity was born for endurance; it is not an exotic, but a hardy plant, braced by the keen wind; not languid, nor childish, nor cowardly. It walks with strong step and erect frame; it is kindly, but firm; it is gentle, but honest; it is calm, but not facile; decided, but not churlish. It does not fear to speak the stern word of condemnation against error, more to raise its voice against surrounding evils, knowing that it is not of this world. It does not shrink from giving honest reproof, lest it come under the charge of displaying an unChristian spirit … The religion of both Old and New Testament is marked by fervent outspoken testimonies against evil. To speak smooth things in such a case may be sentimentalism, but it is not Christianity. It is a betrayal of the cause of truth and righteousness.

If anyone should be frank, mainly honest, cheerful (I do not say blunt or rude, for a Christian must be courteous and polite), it is he who has tasted that the Lord is gracious.

Horatius Bonar

God's Words of Life on
HOPE

Be strong and take heart, all you who hope
in the LORD.

Psalm 31:24

Put your hope in the LORD, for with the LORD
is unfailing love and with him is full redemption.

Psalm 130:7

No one whose hope is in you, O LORD, will
ever be put to shame.

Psalm 25:3

Wait for the LORD; be strong and take heart
and wait for the LORD.

Psalm 27:14

The LORD is good to those whose hope is in
him, to the one who seeks him; it is good to
wait quietly for the salvation of the LORD.

Lamentations 3:25-26

O LORD, my soul faints with longing for your
salvation, but I have put my hope in your
word.

Psalm 119:81

Find rest, O my soul, in God alone; my hope
comes from him. He alone is my rock and
my salvation; he is my fortress, I will not be
shaken.

Psalm 62:5-6

God's Words of Life on
HOPE

You are God my Savior, and my hope is in you all day long.

Psalm 25:5

I wait for the LORD, my soul waits, and in his word I put my hope.

Psalm 130:5

The LORD longs to be gracious to you; he rises to show you compassion. For the LORD is a God of justice. Blessed are all who wait for him!

Isaiah 30:18

May integrity and uprightness protect me, because my hope is in you, O God.

Psalm 25:21

I watch in hope for the LORD, I wait for God my Savior; my God will hear me. Though I have fallen, I will rise. Though I sit in darkness, the LORD will be my light.

Micah 7:7-8

You who fear him, trust in the LORD—he is their help and shield.

Psalm 115:11

You have been my hope, O Sovereign LORD, my confidence since my youth.

Psalm 71:5

God's Words of Life on
HOPE

Why are you downcast, O my soul? Why so disturbed within me? Put your hope in God, for I will yet praise him, my Savior and my God.

Psalm 43:5

Blessed is the man who trusts in the LORD, whose confidence is in him. He will be like a tree planted by the water that sends out its roots by the stream. It does not fear when heat comes; its leaves are always green. It has no worries in a year of drought and never fails to bear fruit.

Jeremiah 17:7–8

Though the fig tree does not bud and there are no grapes on the vines, though the olive crop fails and the yields produce no food, though there are no sheep in the pen and no cattle in the stalls, yet I will rejoice in the LORD, I will be joyful in God my Savior. The Sovereign LORD is my strength; he makes my feet like the feet of a deer, he enables me to go on the heights.

Habakkuk 3:17–19

May your unfailing love rest upon us, O LORD, even as we put our hope in you.

Psalm 33:22

God's Words of Life on
HOPE

O LORD, sustain me according to your promise, and I will live; do not let my hopes be dashed.

Psalm 119:116

Hope deferred makes the heart sick, but a longing fulfilled is a tree of life.

Proverbs 13:12

Blessed is he whose help is the God of Jacob, whose hope is in the LORD his God, the Maker of heaven and earth, the sea, and everything in them—the LORD, who remains faithful forever.

Psalm 146:5–6

This I call to mind and therefore I have hope: Because of the LORD's great love we are not consumed, for his compassions never fail.

Lamentations 3:21–22

Be joyful in hope, patient in affliction, faithful in prayer.

Romans 12:12

I pray also that the eyes of your heart may be enlightened in order that you may know the hope to which Jesus has called you, the riches of his glorious inheritance in the saints.

Ephesians 1:18

God's Words of Life on
HOPE

We wait for the blessed hope—the glorious appearing of our great God and Savior, Jesus Christ.

Titus 2:13

In your hearts set apart Christ as Lord. Always be prepared to give an answer to everyone who asks you to give the reason for the hope that you have.

1 Peter 3:15

Those who hope in the LORD will renew their strength. They will soar on wings like eagles; they will run and not grow weary, they will walk and not be faint.

Isaiah 40:31

Faith is being sure of what we hope for and certain of what we do not see.

Hebrews 11:1

We know that when Christ Jesus appears, we shall be like him, for we shall see him as he is. Everyone who has this hope in him purifies himself, just as he is pure.

1 John 3:2–3

Devotional Thought on
HOPE

It is the wholesome precept of our Lord and Master: "He that endureth," saith he, "unto the end the same shall be saved" (see Matthew 10:22). We must endure and persevere, in order that, being admitted to the hope of truth and liberty, we may attain to the truth and liberty itself; for that very fact that we are Christians is the substance of faith and hope. For we are not following after present glory, but future, according to what Paul the apostle also warns us, and says, "We are saved by hope; but hope that is seen is not hope: for what a man seeth, why doth he hope for? But if we hope for that which we see not, then do we by patience wait for it" (see Romans 8:24). Therefore, waiting and patience are needful, that we may fulfill that which we have begun to be, and may receive that which we believe and hope for, according to God's own showing.

Cyprian

God's Words of Life on
HUMILITY

All of you, clothe yourselves with humility toward one another, because, "God opposes the proud but gives grace to the humble." Humble yourselves, therefore, under God's mighty hand, that he may lift you up in due time.

1 Peter 5:5–6

As God's chosen people, holy and dearly loved, clothe yourselves with compassion, kindness, humility, gentleness and patience.

Colossians 3:12

Jesus said, "Everyone who exalts himself will be humbled, and he who humbles himself will be exalted."

Luke 18:14

He has showed you, O man, what is good. And what does the LORD require of you? To act justly and to love mercy and to walk humbly with your God.

Micah 6:8

The eyes of the arrogant man will be humbled and the pride of men brought low; the LORD alone will be exalted.

Isaiah 2:11

Live in harmony with one another. Do not be proud, but be willing to associate with people of low position. Do not be conceited.

94

Romans 12:16

God's Words of Life on
HUMILITY

A man's pride brings him low, but a man of lowly spirit gains honor.

Proverbs 29:23

God opposes the proud but gives grace to the humble.

James 4:6

The brother in humble circumstances ought to take pride in his high position.

James 1:9

Do nothing out of selfish ambition or vain conceit, but in humility consider others better than yourselves. Each of you should look not only to your own interests, but also to the interests of others.

Philippians 2:3–4

Be completely humble and gentle; be patient, bearing with one another in love.

Ephesians 4:2

Be devoted to one another in brotherly love. Honor one another above yourselves.

Romans 12:10

Jesus replied," Take my yoke upon you and learn from me, for I am gentle and humble in heart, and you will find rest for your souls."

Matthew 11:29   95

God's Words of Life on
HUMILITY

Whoever exalts himself will be humbled, and whoever humbles himself will be exalted.

Matthew 23:12

Jesus replied, "The greatest among you should be like the youngest, and the one who rules like the one who serves. For who is greater, the one who is at the table or the one who serves? Is it not the one who is at the table? But I am among you as one who serves."

Luke 22:26–27

"This is the one I esteem: he who is humble and contrite in spirit, and trembles at my word," says the LORD.

Isaiah 66:2

Humility and the fear of the LORD bring wealth and honor and life.

Proverbs 22:4

The fear of the LORD teaches a man wisdom, and humility comes before honor.

Proverbs 15:33

God guides the humble in what is right and teaches them his way.

Psalm 25:9

Christ must become greater; I must become less.

John 3:30

Devotional Thought on
HUMILITY

Before there can be fullness there must be emptiness. Before God can fill us with himself we must first be emptied of ourselves. It is this emptying that brings the painful disappointment and despair of self of which so many persons have complained just prior to their new and radiant experience.

There must come a total of self-devaluation, a death to all things without us and within us, or there can never be real filling with the Holy Spirit.

While I shy away from "how to" formulas in spiritual things, I believe the answer to the question "How can I be filled?" may be answered in four words, all of them active verbs. They are these: surrender (Romans 12:1-2), ask (Luke 11:13), obey (Acts 5:32), and believe (Galatians 3:2).

Complete and ungrudging obedience to the will of God is absolutely indispensable to the reception of the Spirit's anointing. As we wait before God we should reverently search the Scriptures and listen for the voice of gentle stillness to learn what our heavenly Father expects of us. Then, trusting in his enabling, we should obey to the best of our ability and understanding.

A. W. Tozer

God's Words of Life on
JOY

Consider it pure joy, my brothers, whenever you face trials of many kinds, because you know that the testing of your faith develops perseverance.

James 1:2–3

Rejoice that you participate in the sufferings of Christ, so that you may be overjoyed when his glory is revealed.

1 Peter 4:13

Rejoice in the Lord always. I will say it again: Rejoice!

Philippians 4:4

The kingdom of God is not a matter of eating and drinking, but of righteousness, peace and joy in the Holy Spirit.

Romans 14:17

The fruit of the Spirit is love, joy, peace, patience, kindness, goodness, faithfulness, gentleness and self-control. Against such things there is no law.

Galatians 5:22–23

May the God of hope fill you with all joy and peace as you trust in him, so that you may overflow with hope by the power of the Holy Spirit.

Romans 15:13

God's Words of Life on
JOY

You, O Lord, have made known to me the paths of life; you will fill me with joy in your presence.

Acts 2:28

Ask and you will receive, and your joy will be complete.

John 16:24

There is rejoicing in the presence of the angels of God over one sinner who repents.

Luke 15:10

I delight greatly in the LORD; my soul rejoices in my God. For he has clothed me with garments of salvation and arrayed me in a robe of righteousness.

Isaiah 61:10

Shout for joy, O heavens; rejoice, O earth; burst into song, O mountains! For the LORD comforts his people and will have compassion on his afflicted ones.

Isaiah 49:13

Shout for joy to the LORD, all the earth. Worship the LORD with gladness; come before him with joyful songs.

Psalm 100:1–2

The joy of the LORD is your strength.

Nehemiah 8:10

God's Words of Life on
JOY

The ransomed of the LORD will return. They will enter Zion with singing; everlasting joy will crown their heads. Gladness and joy will overtake them, and sorrow and sighing will flee away.

Isaiah 51:11

Come, let us sing for joy to the LORD; let us shout aloud to the Rock of our salvation. Let us come before him with thanksgiving and extol him with music and song.

Psalm 95:1–2

My lips will shout for joy when I sing praise to you, O LORD—I, whom you have redeemed.

Psalm 71:23

In God our hearts rejoice, for we trust in his holy name.

Psalm 33:21

Weeping may remain for a night, but rejoicing comes in the morning.

Psalm 30:5

The precepts of the LORD are right, giving joy to the heart.

Psalm 19:8

Devotional Thought on
JOY

The joy of the LORD is your strength. Where do the saints get their joy? If we did not know some Christians well, we might think from just observing them that they have no burdens at all to bear. But we must lift the veil from our eyes. The fact that the peace, light, and joy of God is in them is proof that a burden is there as well.

The burden that God places on us squeezes the grapes in our lives and produces the wine, but most of us see only the wine and not the burden. No power on earth or in hell can conquer the Spirit of God living within the human spirit; it creates an inner invincibility. If your life is producing only a whine, instead of the wine, then ruthlessly kick it out. It is definitely a crime for a Christian to be weak in God's strength.

Oswald Chambers

God's Words of Life on
JUSTICE

Jesus said, "You judge by human standards; I pass judgment on no one. But if I do judge, my decisions are right, because I am not alone. I stand with the Father, who sent me."

John 8:15–16

To show partiality in judging is not good: Whoever says to the guilty, "You are innocent"—peoples will curse him and nations denounce him. But it will go well with those who convict the guilty, and rich blessing will come upon them.

Proverbs 24:23–25

Acquitting the guilty and condemning the innocent—the LORD detests them both.

Proverbs 17:15

Defend the cause of the weak and fatherless; maintain the rights of the poor and oppressed. Rescue the weak and needy; deliver them from the hand of the wicked.

Psalm 82:3–4

Do not pervert justice or show partiality. Do not accept a bribe, for a bribe blinds the eyes of the wise and twists the words of the righteous. Follow justice and justice alone, so that you may live.

Deuteronomy 16:19–20

God's Words of Life on
JUSTICE

Do not show partiality in judging; hear both small and great alike. Do not be afraid of any man, for judgment belongs to God.

Deuteronomy 1:17

"These are the things you are to do: Speak the truth to each other, and render true and sound judgment in your courts; do not plot evil against your neighbor, and do not love to swear falsely. I hate all this," declares the LORD.

Zechariah 8:16–17

To do what is right and just is more acceptable to the LORD than sacrifice.

Proverbs 21:3

You must return to your God; maintain love and justice, and wait for your God always.

Hosea 12:6

Seek good, not evil, that you may live. Then the LORD God Almighty will be with you, just as you say he is. Hate evil, love good; maintain justice in the courts.

Amos 5:14–15

This is what the LORD says: "Maintain justice and do what is right, for my salvation is close at hand and my righteousness will soon be revealed."

Isaiah 56:1

God's Words of Life on
JUSTICE

This is what the LORD says: Do what is just and right. Rescue from the hand of his oppressor the one who has been robbed. Do no wrong or violence to the alien, the fatherless or the widow, and do not shed innocent blood in this place.

Jeremiah 22:3

It is from the LORD that man gets justice.

Proverbs 29:6

Love does not delight in evil but rejoices with the truth.

1 Corinthians 13:6

Stop judging by mere appearances, and make a right judgment.

John 7:24

If you show special attention to the man wearing fine clothes and say, "Here's a good seat for you," but say to the poor man, "You stand there" or "Sit on the floor by my feet," have you not discriminated among yourselves and become judges with evil thoughts?

James 2:3–4

It is not good to be partial to the wicked or to deprive the innocent of justice.

Proverbs 18:5

Devotional Thought on
JUSTICE

Anyone who cares about character must care about social conditions, for every unfair economic situation, every social evil left to run its course means ruin to character. The God of the Bible, because he cares supremely for personal life at its best, is zealously in earnest about social justice. His prophets blazed with indignation at all inequity, and his Son made the coming kingdom the center of his message. To fellowship with this earnest purpose of God we all are summoned. He is counting on us to put away the sins that hold the kingdom back and to fight the abuses that crush character in men. To believe in God, therefore—the God who is fighting his way with his children up through ignorance, brutality, and selfishness to a "new heaven and a new earth, the home of righteousness"—is no weakly comfortable blessing (see 2 Peter 3:13). It means joining a moral war; it means devotion, sacrifice. Our underlying assurance that this war for a better world can be won is not simply our belief that it can be done, but our faith that God exists, and that he believes it can be done.

Harry Emerson Fosdick

God's Words of Life on
KINDNESS

Make sure that nobody pays back wrong for wrong, but always try to be kind to each other and to everyone else.

1 Thessalonians 5:15

He who is kind to the poor lends to the LORD, and he will reward him for what he has done.

Proverbs 19:17

He who despises his neighbor sins, but blessed is he who is kind to the needy.

Proverbs 14:21

The fruit of the Spirit is love, joy, peace, patience, kindness, goodness, faithfulness, gentleness and self-control. Against such things there is no law.

Galatians 5:22–23

Our God has not deserted us in our bondage. He has shown us kindness.

Ezra 9:9

"With everlasting kindness I will have compassion on you," says the LORD your Redeemer.

Isaiah 54:8

God's Words of Life on
KINDNESS

"I am the LORD, who exercises kindness, justice and righteousness on earth, for in these I delight," declares the LORD.

Jeremiah 9:24

God has shown kindness by giving you rain from heaven and crops in their seasons; he provides you with plenty of food and fills your hearts with joy.

Acts 14:17

Consider therefore the kindness and sternness of God: sternness to those who fell, but kindness to you, provided that you continue in his kindness.

Romans 11:22

Therefore, as God's chosen people, holy and dearly loved, clothe yourselves with compassion, kindness, humility, gentleness and patience.

Colossians 3:12

When the kindness and love of God our Savior appeared, he saved us, not because of righteous things we had done, but because of his mercy.

Titus 3:4–5

Love is patient, love is kind. It does not envy, it does not boast, it is not proud.

1 Corinthians 13:4

God's Words of Life on
KINDNESS

Make every effort to add to your faith goodness; and to goodness, knowledge; and to knowledge, self-control; and to self-control, perseverance; and to perseverance, godliness; and to godliness, brotherly kindness; and to brotherly kindness, love. For if you possess these qualities in increasing measure, they will keep you from being ineffective and unproductive in your knowledge of our Lord Jesus Christ.

2 Peter 1:5–8

We who are strong ought to bear with the failings of the weak and not to please ourselves. Each of us should please his neighbor for his good, to build him up.

Romans 15:1–2

May kindness and faithfulness be with you.

2 Samuel 15:20

Be kind and compassionate to one another, forgiving each other, just as in Christ God forgave you.

Ephesians 4:32

Devotional Thought on
KINDNESS

It is Christ who pines when the poor are hungry; it is Christ who is repulsed when strangers are not welcome; it is Christ who suffers when rags fail to keep out the cold; it is Christ who is in anguish in the long-drawn illness; it is Christ who waits behind the prison doors. You come upon one of those who have been broken by the tempests of life, and if you look with eyes of Christian faith and love, you will know that you are standing before the King of kings, and Lord of lords. Civilization, as we know it, produces much human refuse. Slum dwellings, long hours of work, underpayment, child labor, lack of education, prostitution—all these evils are responsible for stunting and warping the development of souls. Unless we are exerting all the strength that Christ gives us in ending these bad conditions, then the responsibility for wasted lives lies at our door, and from the streets of cities or the lanes of countrysides the cry goes up through the lips of their Savior and our Judge: "Whatever you did not do for one of the least of these, you did not do for me."

William Temple

God's Words of Life on
LOVE

Love is patient, love is kind. It does not envy, it does not boast, it is not proud. It is not rude, it is not self-seeking, it is not easily angered, it keeps no record of wrongs. Love does not delight in evil but rejoices with the truth. It always protects, always trusts, always hopes, always perseveres. Love never fails.

1 Corinthians 13:4–8

God did not give us a spirit of timidity, but a spirit of power, of love and of self-discipline.

2 Timothy 1:7

No one has ever seen God; but if we love one another, God lives in us and his love is made complete in us.

1 John 4:12

God is love. Whoever lives in love lives in God, and God in him.

1 John 4:16

Do not seek revenge or bear a grudge against one of your people, but love your neighbor as yourself.

Leviticus 19:18

He who covers over an offense promotes love, but whoever repeats the matter separates close friends.

Proverbs 17:9

God's Words of Life on
LOVE

You have heard that it was said, "Love your neighbor and hate your enemy." But I tell you: Love your enemies and pray for those who persecute you, that you may be sons of your Father in heaven.

Matthew 5:43–44

A new command I give you: Love one another. As I have loved you, so you must love one another. By this all men will know that you are my disciples, if you love one another.

John 13:34–35

Jesus replied, "My command is this: Love each other as I have loved you. Greater love has no one than this, that he lay down his life for his friends."

John 15:12–13

Knowledge puffs up, but love builds up.

1 Corinthians 8:1

This is my prayer: that your love may abound more and more in knowledge and depth of insight, so that you may be able to discern what is best and may be pure and blameless until the day of Christ.

Philippians 1:9-10

God's Words of Life on
LOVE

Pursue righteousness, faith, love and peace, along with those who call on the Lord out of a pure heart.

2 Timothy 2:22

The fruit of the Spirit is love, joy, peace, patience, kindness, goodness, faithfulness, gentleness and self-control. Against such things there is no law.

Galatians 5:22–23

If anyone obeys his word, God's love is truly made complete in him.

1 John 2:5

Live in harmony with one another; be sympathetic, love as brothers, be compassionate and humble.

1 Peter 3:8

Let us love one another, for love comes from God. Everyone who loves has been born of God and knows God. Whoever does not love does not know God, because God is love. This is how God showed his love among us: He sent his one and only Son into the world that we might live through him. This is love: not that we loved God, but that he loved us and sent his Son as an atoning sacrifice for our sins. Dear friends, since God so loved us, we also ought to love one another.

1 John 4:7–11

God's Words of Life on
LOVE

If you really keep the royal law found in Scripture, "Love your neighbor as yourself," you are doing right.

James 2:8

Make my joy complete by being like-minded, having the same love, being one in spirit and purpose.

Philippians 2:2

Make every effort to add to your faith goodness; and to goodness, knowledge; and to knowledge, self-control; and to self-control, perseverance; and to perseverance, godliness; and to godliness, brotherly kindness; and to brotherly kindness, love.

2 Peter 1:5-7

If anyone says, "I love God," yet hates his brother, he is a liar. For anyone who does not love his brother, whom he has seen, cannot love God, whom he has not seen. And he has given us this command: Whoever loves God must also love his brother.

1 John 4:20-21

Do everything in love.

1 Corinthians 16:14

God's Words of Life on
LOVE

Love each other deeply, because love covers over a multitude of sins.

1 Peter 4:8

Whoever loves his brother lives in the light, and there is nothing in him to make him stumble.

1 John 2:10

Let us not love with words or tongue but with actions and in truth.

1 John 3:18

Hatred stirs up dissension, but love covers over all wrongs.

Proverbs 10:12

He has taken me to the banquet hall, and his banner over me is love.

Song of Songs 2:4

This is love: that we walk in obedience to God's commands. As you have heard from the beginning, his command is that you walk in love.

2 John 6

Devotional Thought on
LOVE

The law of love is good and sweet. It is not only borne lightly and easily, but it also makes bearable the laws which make men into slaves and hirelings. It does not destroy them; it fulfills them. As the Lord says, "I have not come to take away the law but to fulfill it" (Matthew 5:17). It tempers the slave's law and makes the hireling's law orderly. It lightens both. For there will never be any love without fear but chaste love. There will never be love without greed unless it is kept within bounds. Therefore love fulfills the slave's law when it overflows in devotion. It fulfills the hireling's law when it sets limits to greed.

Greed is brought to order when love overshadows it and evils are condemned and what is better is preferred to what is merely good, and the good desired only for the sake of what is better. When by the grace of God this is fully achieved, the body is loved, and all the goods of the body for the sake of the soul, and the goods of the soul for the sake of God, and God for his own sake.

Bernard of Clairvaux

God's Words of Life on
LOVING GOD

Love the LORD your God with all your heart and with all your soul and with all your strength.

Deuteronomy 6:5

What does the LORD your God ask of you but to fear the LORD your God, to walk in all his ways, to love him, to serve the LORD your God with all your heart and with all your soul.

Deuteronomy 10:12

Love the LORD your God, then you will live and increase, and the LORD your God will bless you.

Deuteronomy 30:16

Love the LORD your God, listen to his voice, and hold fast to him. For the LORD is your life.

Deuteronomy 30:20

Be very careful to keep the commandment and the law that Moses the servant of the LORD gave you: to love the LORD your God, to walk in all his ways, to obey his commands, to hold fast to him and to serve him with all your heart and all your soul.

Joshua 22:5

The man who loves God is known by God.

1 Corinthians 8:3

God's Words of Life on
LOVING GOD

We know that in all things God works for the good of those who love him, who have been called according to his purpose.

Romans 8:28

To love the Lord with all your heart, with all your understanding and with all your strength, and to love your neighbor as yourself is more important than all burnt offerings and sacrifices.

Mark 12:33

Hear, O Israel, the Lord our God, the Lord is one. Love the Lord your God with all your heart and with all your soul and with all your mind and with all your strength.

Mark 12:29–30

I love you, O LORD, my strength. The LORD is my rock, my fortress and my deliverer; my God is my rock, in whom I take refuge. He is my shield and the horn of my salvation, my stronghold.

Psalm 18:1–2

"Because he loves me," says the LORD, "I will rescue him; I will protect him, for he acknowledges my name."

Psalm 91:14

God's Words of Life on
LOVING GOD

Be very careful to love the LORD your God.

Joshua 23:11

Let those who love the LORD hate evil, for he guards the lives of his faithful ones and delivers them from the hand of the wicked.

Psalm 97:10

Jesus said to them, "If God were your Father, you would love me, for I came from God and now am here. I have not come on my own; but he sent me."

John 8:42

Praise be to the LORD my Rock. He is my loving God and my fortress, my stronghold and my deliverer, my shield, in whom I take refuge.

Psalm 144:1-2

Blessed is the man who perseveres under trial, because when he has stood the test, he will receive the crown of life that God has promised to those who love him.

James 1:12

Devotional Thought on
LOVING GOD

Let us all love with all our heart, with all our soul, with all our mind, with all our strength and fortitude, with all our understanding and with all our powers, with our whole might and whole affection, with our innermost parts, our whole desires, and wills, the Lord God, who has given and gives to us all, the whole body, the whole soul, and our life; who has created and redeemed us, and by his mercy alone will save us; who has done and does all good to us, miserable and wretched, vile, unclean, ungrateful, and evil.

Let us therefore desire nothing else, wish for nothing else, and let nothing please and delight us except our Creator and Redeemer, and Savior, the only true God, who is full of good, who alone is good, merciful and kind, gentle and sweet, who alone is holy, just, true, and upright, who alone is benign, pure, and clean, from whom, and through whom, and in whom is all mercy, all grace, all glory of all penitents and of the just, and of all the blessed rejoicing in heaven. Let nothing therefore hinder us, let nothing separate us, let nothing come between us.

St. Francis of Assisi   119

God's Words of Life on
MERCY

Mercy triumphs over judgment!

James 2:13

Get rid of all bitterness, rage and anger, brawling and slander, along with every form of malice. Be kind and compassionate to one another, forgiving each other, just as in Christ God forgave you.

Ephesians 4:31–32

Blessed are the merciful, for they will be shown mercy.

Matthew 5:7

The wisdom that comes from heaven is first of all pure; then peace-loving, considerate, submissive, full of mercy and good fruit, impartial and sincere.

James 3:17

Let us then approach the throne of grace with confidence, so that we may receive mercy and find grace to help us in our time of need.

Hebrews 4:16

Turn to me and have mercy on me, as you always do to those who love your name. Direct my footsteps, O Lord, according to your word; let no sin rule over me.

Psalm 119:132-133

Devotional Thought on
MERCY

Merciful Lord, it does not surprise me that you forget completely the sins of those who repent. I am not surprised that you remain faithful to those who hate and revile you. The mercy which pours forth from you fills the whole world.

It was by your mercy that we were created, and by your mercy that you redeemed us by sending your Son. Your mercy is the light in which sinners find you and good people come back to you. Your mercy is everywhere, even in the depths of hell where you offer to forgive the tortured souls. Your justice is constantly tempered with mercy, so you refuse to punish us as we deserve. It was not enough for you to take on our humanity; you had to die for us as well.

Catherine of Siena

God's Words of Life on
OBEDIENCE

This is love: that we walk in obedience to his commands. As you have heard from the beginning, his command is that you walk in love.

2 John 6

We know that we have come to know him if we obey his commands. The man who says, "I know him," but does not do what he commands is a liar, and the truth is not in him. But if anyone obeys his word, God's love is truly made complete in him.

1 John 2:3–5

Blessed are they who keep God's statutes and seek him with all their heart.

Psalm 119:2

Does the LORD delight in burnt offerings and sacrifices as much as in obeying the voice of the LORD? To obey is better than sacrifice, and to heed is better than the fat of rams.

1 Samuel 15:22

I have considered my ways and have turned my steps to your statutes, O LORD. I will hasten and not delay to obey your commands.

Psalm 119:59–60

God's Words of Life on
OBEDIENCE

He who obeys instructions guards his life, but he who is contemptuous of his ways will die.

Proverbs 19:16

Obey me, and I will be your God and you will be my people. Walk in all the ways I command you, that it may go well with you.

Jeremiah 7:23

If our hearts do not condemn us, we have confidence before God and receive from him anything we ask, because we obey his commands and do what pleases him.

1 John 3:21–22

Jesus said, "If you obey my commands, you will remain in my love, just as I have obeyed my Father's commands and remain in his love."

John 15:10

Blessed are those who hear the word of God and obey it.

Luke 11:28

We must obey God rather than men!

Acts 5:29

Do not merely listen to the word, and so deceive yourselves. Do what it says.

James 1:22–24

God's Words of Life on
OBEDIENCE

To love God with all your heart, with all your understanding and with all your strength, and to love your neighbor as yourself is more important than all burnt offerings and sacrifices.

Mark 12:33

Jesus replied, "If anyone loves me, he will obey my teaching. My Father will love him, and we will come to him and make our home with him. He who does not love me will not obey my teaching. These words you hear are not my own; they belong to the Father who sent me.

John 14:23-24

"Obey me and do everything I command you, and you will be my people, and I will be your God," says the LORD.

Jeremiah 11:4

Be very careful to keep the commandment and the law that Moses the servant of the LORD gave you: to love the LORD your God, to walk in all his ways, to obey his commands, to hold fast to him and to serve him with all your heart and all your soul.

Joshua 22:5

Devotional Thought on
OBEDIENCE

Whosoever keeps the whole law yet offends at one point is guilty of all (see James 2:10). He is rightly subject to the whole penalty. If he habitually disobeys God in one thing, then he doesn't obey him in anything, because obedience to God consists in an attitude of the heart. It is willingness to obey God, to let him rule everything. So if a person habitually disobeys God in one thing, his state of heart renders obedience in anything else impossible, because a person can't in one area obey God out of respect for his authority while in another area refuse obedience.

Obedience to God is an obedient state of heart, a preference for God's authority and commandments over everything else. If a person therefore appears to obey in some areas yet he knowingly disobeys in others, he is deceived. He offends in one point, and this proves he is guilty of all; in others words, he doesn't obey from the heart at all. If a person refuses to obey God's law, even a single duty, he has no true faith, and his outwardly spiritual acts are loathsome.

Charles G. Finney

God's Words of Life on
PATIENCE

Be still before the LORD and wait patiently for him; do not fret when men succeed in their ways.

Psalm 37:7

A patient man calms a quarrel.

Proverbs 15:18

Everyone should be quick to listen, slow to speak and slow to become angry, for man's anger does not bring about the righteous life that God desires.

James 1:19–20

The end of a matter is better than its beginning, and patience is better than pride.

Ecclesiastes 7:8–9

To those who by persistence in doing good seek glory, honor and immortality, God will give eternal life.

Romans 2:7

We also rejoice in our sufferings, because we know that suffering produces perseverance; perseverance, character; and character, hope.

Romans 5:3–4

Be joyful in hope, patient in affliction, faithful in prayer.

Romans 12:12

God's Words of Life on
PATIENCE

Wait for the LORD; be strong and take heart and wait for the LORD.

Psalm 27:14

You need to persevere so that when you have done the will of God, you will receive what he has promised.

Hebrews 10:36

Since we are surrounded by such a great cloud of witnesses, let us throw off everything that hinders and the sin that so easily entangles, and let us run with perseverance the race marked out for us.

Hebrews 12:1

Let us not become weary in doing good, for at the proper time we will reap a harvest if we do not give up.

Galatians 6:9

Be completely humble and gentle; be patient, bearing with one another in love.

Ephesians 4:2

The fruit of the Spirit is love, joy, peace, patience, kindness, goodness, faithfulness, gentleness and self-control. Against such things there is no law.

Galatians 5:22–23

God's Words of Life on
PATIENCE

Encourage the timid, help the weak, be patient with everyone.

1 Thessalonians 5:14

The LORD longs to be gracious to you; he rises to show you compassion. For the LORD is a God of justice. Blessed are all who wait for him!

Isaiah 30:18

As God's chosen people, holy and dearly loved, clothe yourselves with compassion, kindness, humility, gentleness and patience. Bear with each other and forgive whatever grievances you may have against one another. Forgive as the Lord forgave you. And over all these virtues put on love, which binds them all together in perfect unity.

Colossians 3:12

The Lord is not slow in keeping his promise, as some understand slowness. He is patient with you, not wanting anyone to perish, but everyone to come to repentance.

2 Peter 3:9

You, O LORD, are a compassionate and gracious God, slow to anger, abounding in love and faithfulness.

Psalm 86:15

Devotional Thought on
PATIENCE

It may seem an easy thing to wait, but it is one of the postures which a Christian soldier does not learn without years of teaching. There are hours of perplexity when the most willing spirit, anxiously desirous to serve the Lord, knows not what part to take. Then what shall it do? Vex itself by despair? Fly back in cowardice, turn to the right hand in fear, or rush forward in presumption? No, simply wait.

Wait in prayer, however. Call on God, and spread the case before him; tell him your difficulty and plead his promise of aid. In dilemmas between one duty and another, it is sweet to be humble as a child and wait with simplicity of soul on the Lord. It is sure to be well with us when we feel and know our own folly, and are heartily willing to be guided by the will of God.

But wait in faith. Express your unstaggering confidence in him, for unfaithful, untrusting waiting is but an insult to the Lord. Believe that if he keeps you tarrying even till midnight, yet he will come at the right time; the vision will come and will not tarry.

Charles H. Spurgeon

God's Words of Life on
PEACE

Blessed are the peacemakers, for they will be called sons of God.

Matthew 5:9

Aim for perfection, listen to my appeal, be of one mind, live in peace. And the God of love and peace will be with you.

2 Corinthians 13:11

If it is possible, as far as it depends on you, live at peace with everyone.

Romans 12:18

Pursue righteousness, faith, love and peace, along with those who call on the Lord out of a pure heart.

2 Timothy 2:22

Let the peace of Christ rule in your hearts, since as members of one body you were called to peace. And be thankful.

Colossians 3:15

The fruit of the Spirit is love, joy, peace, patience, kindness, goodness, faithfulness, gentleness and self-control. Against such things there is no law.

Galatians 5:22–23

God is not a God of disorder but of peace.

1 Corinthians 14:33

God's Words of Life on
PEACE

Let us therefore make every effort to do what leads to peace and to mutual edification.

Romans 14:19

Turn from evil and do good; seek peace and pursue it.

Psalm 34:14

Do not be anxious about anything, but in everything, by prayer and petition, with thanksgiving, present your requests to God. And the peace of God, which transcends all understanding, will guard your hearts and your minds in Christ Jesus.

Philippians 4:6–7

May the God of hope fill you with all joy and peace as you trust in him, so that you may overflow with hope by the power of the Holy Spirit.

Romans 15:13

The mind of sinful man is death, but the mind controlled by the Spirit is life and peace.

Romans 8:6

Jesus said, "Peace I leave with you; my peace I give you. I do not give to you as the world gives. Do not let your hearts be troubled and do not be afraid."

John 14:27

God's Words of Life on
PEACE

When a man's ways are pleasing to the LORD, he makes even his enemies live at peace with him.

Proverbs 16:7

May the Lord of peace himself give you peace at all times and in every way.

2 Thessalonians 3:16

The fruit of righteousness will be peace; the effect of righteousness will be quietness and confidence forever.

Isaiah 32:17

You will keep in perfect peace him whose mind is steadfast, because he trusts in you.

Isaiah 26:3

Great peace have they who love your law, O LORD, and nothing can make them stumble.

Psalm 119:165

The LORD gives strength to his people; the LORD blesses his people with peace.

Psalm 29:11

The LORD bless you and keep you; the LORD make his face shine upon you and be gracious to you; the LORD turn his face toward you and give you peace.

Numbers 6:24–26

Devotional Thought on
PEACE

Now as they were going along and talking, they espied a boy feeding his father's sheep. The boy was in very mean clothes, but of a very fresh and well-favored countenance, and as he sat by himself he sang. Hark, said Mr. Greatheart, to what the shepherd's boy saith. So they hearkened, and he said:

He that is down needs fear no fall, he that is low no pride:

He that is humble ever shall have God to be his guide.

I am content with what I have, little be it or much:

And, Lord, contentment still I crave, because thou savest such.

Fullness to such a burden is that go on pilgrimage:

Here little, and hereafter bliss, is best from age to age.

Then said their guide, Do you hear him? I will dare to say that this boy lives a merrier life, and wears more of that herb called hearts-ease in his bosom, than he that is clad in silk and velvet.

John Bunyan

God's Words of Life on
PERSEVERANCE

The righteous will hold to their ways, and those with clean hands will grow stronger.

Job 17:9

If the LORD delights in a man's way, he makes his steps firm; though he stumble, he will not fall, for the LORD upholds him with his hand.

Psalm 37:23–24

Return to your God; maintain love and justice, and wait for your God always.

Hosea 12:6

Jesus said, "All men will hate you because of me, but he who stands firm to the end will be saved."

Matthew 10:22

Be faithful, even to the point of death, and I will give you the crown of life.

Revelation 2:10

To him who overcomes, I will give the right to eat from the tree of life, which is in the paradise of God.

Revelation 2:7

Let us not become weary in doing good, for at the proper time we will reap a harvest if we do not give up.

Galatians 6:9

God's Words of Life on
PERSEVERANCE

Blessed is the man who perseveres under trial, because when he has stood the test, he will receive the crown of life that God has promised to those who love him.

James 1:12

To those who by persistence in doing good seek glory, honor and immortality, God will give eternal life.

Romans 2:7

Jesus taught them saying, "Remain in me, and I will remain in you. No branch can bear fruit by itself; it must remain in the vine. Neither can you bear fruit unless you remain in me. I am the vine; you are the branches. If a man remains in me and I in him, he will bear much fruit; apart from me you can do nothing."

John 15:4–5

I am convinced that neither death nor life, neither angels nor demons, neither the present nor the future, nor any powers, neither height nor depth, nor anything else in all creation, will be able to separate us from the love of God that is in Christ Jesus our Lord.

Romans 8:38–39

Be on your guard; stand firm in the faith.

1 Corinthians 16:13

God's Words of Life on
PERSEVERANCE

He will keep you strong to the end, so that
you will be blameless on the day of our Lord
Jesus Christ. God, who has called you into
fellowship with his Son Jesus Christ our
Lord, is faithful.

1 Corinthians 1:8–9

Stand firm. Let nothing move you. Always
give yourselves fully to the work of the Lord,
because you know that your labor in the
Lord is not in vain.

1 Corinthians 15:58

Be on your guard so that you may not be
carried away by the error of lawless men and
fall from your secure position. But grow in
the grace and knowledge of our Lord and
Savior Jesus Christ. To him be glory both
now and forever! Amen.

2 Peter 3:17–18

Put on the full armor of God, so that when
the day of evil comes, you may be able to
stand your ground, and after you have done
everything, to stand. Stand firm then, with
the belt of truth buckled around your waist,
with the breastplate of righteousness in
place, and with your feet fitted with the
readiness that comes from the gospel of
peace.

Ephesians 6:13–15

God's Words of Life on
PERSEVERANCE

God who began a good work in you will carry it on to completion until the day of Christ Jesus.

Philippians 1:6

May our Lord Jesus Christ himself and God our Father, who loved us and by his grace gave us eternal encouragement and good hope, encourage your hearts and strengthen you in every good deed and word.

2 Thessalonians 2:16–17

Never tire of doing what is right.

2 Thessalonians 3:13

Be self-controlled and alert. Your enemy the devil prowls around like a roaring lion looking for someone to devour.

1 Peter 5:8

We must pay more careful attention, therefore, to what we have heard, so that we do not drift away.

Hebrews 2:1

You will have success if you are careful to observe the decrees and laws that the LORD gave Moses for Israel. Be strong and courageous. Do not be afraid or discouraged.

1 Chronicles 22:13

God's Words of Life on
PERSEVERANCE

"Keep my commands and you will live;
guard my teachings as the apple of your eye,"
says the LORD.

Proverbs 7:2

Do not throw away your confidence; it will
be richly rewarded. You need to persevere so
that when you have done the will of God,
you will receive what he has promised.

Hebrews 10:35–36

Perseverance must finish its work so that you
may be mature and complete, not lacking
anything.

James 1:4

The man who looks intently into the perfect
law that gives freedom, and continues to do
this, not forgetting what he has heard, but
doing it—he will be blessed in what he does.

James 1:25

Let him who does right continue to do right;
and let him who is holy continue to be holy.
Behold, I am coming soon! My reward is
with me, and I will give to everyone
according to what he has done.

Revelation 22:11–12

Devotional Thought on
PERSEVERANCE

So long as we live in this world we cannot be without tribulation and temptation. Everyone therefore ought to watch in prayer, lest the devil find an occasion to deceive him; who never sleepeth, but goeth about seeking whom he may devour (see 1 Peter 5:8). No man is so perfect and holy, but he hath sometimes temptations. Nevertheless, temptations are often very profitable to us, for in them a man is humbled, purified, and instructed.

All saints passed through many tribulations and temptations. They that could not bear temptations fell away. There is no order so holy, nor place so secret, where there be not temptations, or adversities. Some suffer great temptations in the beginning of their conversion; others at the end; still others almost through the whole of their life.

We ought not therefore to despair when we are tempted, but so much the more fervently to pray unto God, who surely will give with the temptation a way of escape, that we may be able to bear it. Let us therefore humble our soul under the hand of God in all temptations and tribulations, for he will save and exalt the humble in spirit.

Thomas à Kempis

God's Words of Life on
PERSPECTIVE

Set your minds on things above, not on earthly things.

Colossians 3:2

"For my thoughts are not your thoughts, neither are your ways my ways," declares the LORD. "As the heavens are higher than the earth, so are my ways higher than your ways and my thoughts than your thoughts."

Isaiah 55:8–9

There is a time for everything, and a season for every activity under heaven: a time to be born and a time to die, a time to plant and a time to uproot, a time to kill and a time to heal, a time to tear down and a time to build, a time to weep and a time to laugh, a time to mourn and a time to dance, a time to scatter stones and a time to gather them, a time to embrace and a time to refrain, a time to search and a time to give up, a time to keep and a time to throw away, a time to tear and a time to mend, a time to be silent and a time to speak, a time to love and a time to hate, a time for war and a time for peace.

Ecclesiastes 3:1–8

"I know the plans I have for you," declares the LORD, "plans to prosper you and not to harm you, plans to give you hope and a future."

Jeremiah 29:11

Devotional Thought on
PERSPECTIVE

For disappointments that come not by our own folly, they are the trials or corrections of heaven. It is our own fault if they prove not to our advantage. To see the hand of God in them, with a humble submission to his will, is the way to turn our water into wine and engage the greatest love and mercy on our side.

If we look only at our losses, consider how little we deserve what is left. Our passion will cool, and our murmurs will turn into thankfulness.

In him, his humble, sincere disciples find more than all that they lose in the world. All we have is the Almighty's; and shall not God have his own when he calls for it?

Discontentedness is not only in such a case ingratitude, but injustice. For we are both unthankful for the time we had it, and not honest enough to restore it, if we could keep it.

But it is hard for us to look on things in such a glass, and at such a distance from this low world; and yet it is our duty, and would be our wisdom and our glory to do so.

William Penn

God's Words of Life on
PRAYER

"Before they call I will answer; while they are still speaking I will hear," says the LORD.

Isaiah 65:24

Whatever you ask for in prayer, believe that you have received it, and it will be yours.

Mark 11:24

Ask and it will be given to you; seek and you will find; knock and the door will be opened to you. For everyone who asks receives; he who seeks finds; and to him who knocks, the door will be opened.

Matthew 7:7–8

Jesus said, "I tell you that if two of you on earth agree about anything you ask for, it will be done for you by my Father in heaven. For where two or three come together in my name, there am I with them."

Matthew 18:19–20

If our hearts do not condemn us, we have confidence before God and receive from him anything we ask, because we obey his commands and do what pleases him.

1 John 3:21–22

I wait for you, O LORD; you will answer, O Lord, my God.

Psalm 38:15

God's Words of Life on
PRAYER

"Call to me and I will answer you and tell you great and unsearchable things you do not know," says the LORD.

Jeremiah 33:3

Let us then approach the throne of grace with confidence, so that we may receive mercy and find grace to help us in our time of need.

Hebrews 4:16

Jesus answered, "I tell you the truth, my Father will give you whatever you ask in my name. Until now you have not asked for anything in my name. Ask and you will receive, and your joy will be complete."

John 16:23–24

"If my people, who are called by my name, will humble themselves and pray and seek my face and turn from their wicked ways, then will I hear from heaven and will forgive their sin and will heal their land," says the Lord.

2 Chronicles 7:14

This is the confidence we have in approaching God: that if we ask anything according to his will, he hears us. And if we know that he hears us—whatever we ask—we know that we have what we asked of him.

1 John 5:14–15

God's Words of Life on
PRAYER

Jesus taught them saying, "When you pray, do not be like the hypocrites, for they love to pray standing in the synagogues and on the street corners to be seen by men. I tell you the truth, they have received their reward in full. But when you pray, go into your room, close the door and pray to your Father, who is unseen. Then your Father, who sees what is done in secret, will reward you."

Matthew 6:5–6

Is any one of you in trouble? He should pray. Is anyone happy? Let him sing songs of praise. Is any one of you sick? He should call the elders of the church to pray over him and anoint him with oil in the name of the Lord. And the prayer offered in faith will make the sick person well; the Lord will raise him up. If he has sinned, he will be forgiven. Therefore confess your sins to each other and pray for each other so that you may be healed. The prayer of a righteous man is powerful and effective.

James 5:13–16

For the eyes of the Lord are on the righteous and his ears are attentive to their prayer.

1 Peter 3:12

Devotional Thought on
PRAYER

Private prayer does not require any special place. Jesus Christ, indeed, commands us when we pray to enter into our chamber and close the door, and so to pray secretly unto our Father (see Matthew 6:6). By this he means that we should choose for our prayers such places as will offer least distraction. Jesus Christ himself observed no special place of prayer. We find him sometimes praying on the Mount of Olives, sometimes in the desert, sometimes in the temple, and also in the Garden of Gethsemane. Peter prayed on a housetop. Paul prayed in prison and was heard of God; and he commands men to pray in all places.

But public prayers should be made in places appointed for the assembling of Christians; and it is inexcusable willfully to absent oneself from these exercises of worship. I do not mean that to be absent from that particular place is sinful, but the promise clearly made that, "For where two or three are gathered together in my name, there am I in the midst of them" (Matthew 18:20, KJV), condemns all those who neglect to join the congregation gathered in his name.

John Knox

God's Words of Life on
HIS PRESENCE

Jesus said, "And surely I am with you always, to the very end of the age."

Matthew 28:20

For the sake of his great name the LORD will not reject his people, because the LORD was pleased to make you his own.

1 Samuel 12:22

Do not fear, for I am with you; do not be dismayed, for I am your God. I will strengthen you and help you; I will uphold you with my righteous right hand.

Isaiah 41:10

The eternal God is your refuge, and underneath are the everlasting arms.

Deuteronomy 33:27

Be strong and courageous. Do not be afraid or terrified because of them, for the LORD your God goes with you; he will never leave you nor forsake you.

Deuteronomy 31:6

Those who know your name will trust in you, for you, LORD, have never forsaken those who seek you.

Psalm 9:10

God's Words of Life on
HIS PRESENCE

Who shall separate us from the love of Christ? Shall trouble or hardship or persecution or famine or nakedness or danger or sword? As it is written: "For your sake we face death all day long; we are considered as sheep to be slaughtered." No, in all these things we are more than conquerors through him who loved us. For I am convinced that neither death nor life, neither angels nor demons, neither the present nor the future, nor any powers, neither height nor depth, nor anything else in all creation, will be able to separate us from the love of God that is in Christ Jesus our LORD.

Romans 8:35–39

God is our refuge and strength, an ever-present help in trouble.

Psalm 46:1

Where can I go from your Spirit? Where can I flee from your presence? If I go up to the heavens, you are there; if I make my bed in the depths, you are there. If I rise on the wings of the dawn, if I settle on the far side of the sea, even there your hand will guide me, your right hand will hold me fast.

Psalm 139:7–10

God's Words of Life on
HIS PRESENCE

"You will seek me and find me when you seek me with all your heart," says the LORD.

Jeremiah 29:13

How great is your goodness, which you have stored up for those who fear you, which you bestow in the sight of men on those who take refuge in you. In the shelter of your presence you hide them from the intrigues of men; in your dwelling you keep them safe.

Psalm 31:19–20

"He will call upon me, and I will answer him; I will be with him in trouble, I will deliver him and honor him. With long life will I satisfy him and show him my salvation," says the LORD.

Psalm 91:15–16

"See, I have engraved you on the palms of my hands," says the LORD.

Isaiah 49:16

He will not let your foot slip—he who watches over you will not slumber. The LORD watches over you—the LORD is your shade at your right hand; the sun will not harm you by day, nor the moon by night. The LORD will keep you from all harm—he will watch over your life; the LORD will watch over your
148 coming and going both now and forevermore.

Psalm 121:3, 5–8

Devotional Thought on
GOD'S PRESENCE

There is no sweeter manner of living in the world than continuous communion with God. If I were a preacher, I would preach nothing but practicing the presence of God. If I were to be responsible for guiding souls in the right direction, I would urge everyone to be aware of God's constant presence, if for no other reason than because his presence is a delight to our souls and spirits.

It is, however, also necessary. If we only knew how much we need God's grace, we would never lose touch with him. Believe me. Make a commitment never to deliberately stray from him, to live the rest of your life in his holy presence. Don't do this in expectation of receiving heavenly comforts; simply do it out of love for him.

Put your hand to the task! If you do it right, you will soon see the results.

Brother Lawrence

God's Words of Life on
PRIDE

A man's pride brings him low, but a man of lowly spirit gains honor.

Proverbs 29:23

Patience is better than pride.

Ecclesiastes 7:8

Pride goes before destruction, a haughty spirit before a fall.

Proverbs 16:18

When pride comes, then comes disgrace, but with humility comes wisdom.

Proverbs 11:2

Pride only breeds quarrels, but wisdom is found in those who take advice.

Proverbs 13:10

Each one should test his own actions. Then he can take pride in himself, without comparing himself to somebody else.

Galatians 6:4

Everyone who exalts himself will be humbled, and he who humbles himself will be exalted.

Luke 18:14

Devotional Thought on
PRIDE

It is pride which has been the chief cause of misery in every nation and every family since the world began. Other vices may sometimes bring people together: you may find good fellowship and jokes and friendliness among drunken people or unchaste people. But pride always means enmity—it is enmity. And not only enmity between man and man, but enmity to God.

In God you come up against something which is in every respect immeasurably superior to yourself. Unless you know God as that—and, therefore, know yourself as nothing in comparison—you do not know God at all. As long as you are proud you cannot know God. A proud man is always looking down on things and people: and, of course, as long as you are looking down, you cannot see something that is above you.

C. S. Lewis

God's Words of Life on
SERVANTHOOD

Be devoted to one another in brotherly love.
Honor one another above yourselves. Never
be lacking in zeal, but keep your spiritual
fervor, serving the Lord.

Romans 12:10–11

Jesus said, "The greatest among you will be
your servant."

Matthew 23:11

If serving the LORD seems undesirable to you,
then choose for yourselves this day whom
you will serve. But as for me and my household, we will serve the LORD.

Joshua 24:15

Be sure to fear the LORD and serve him faithfully with all your heart; consider what great
things he has done for you.

1 Samuel 12:24

If anyone serves, he should do it with the
strength God provides, so that in all things
God may be praised through Jesus Christ. To
him be the glory and the power for ever and
ever. Amen.

1 Peter 4:11

Devotional Thought on
SERVANTHOOD

Our religion lay not in meats, nor drinks, nor clothes, nor thee nor thou, nor putting off hats nor making curtseys (at which they were greatly offended because we thee'd and thou'd them and could not put off our hats nor bow to them), and therefore they said our religion lay in such things. But our answer was, "Nay; for though the Spirit of God led into that which was comely and decent, and from chambering and wantonness, and from sporting and pastimes and feasting as in the day of slaughter, and from wearing costly apparel—our religion lies in that which brings to visit the poor, and fatherless, and widows, and keeps from the spots of the world (which religion is pure and undefiled before God [see James 1:27]). This is our religion which we own, which the apostles were in above 1600 years since; and we do deny all vain religions got up since, which are not only spotted with the world, but plead for a body of sin and death to the grave; and their widows and fatherless lie begging up and down the streets and countries."

George Fox

God's Words of Life on
SIN & TEMPTATION

I acknowledged my sin to you and did not cover up my iniquity. I said, "I will confess my transgressions to the LORD"—and you forgave the guilt of my sin.

Psalm 32:5

For all have sinned and fall short of the glory of God.

Romans 3:23

There is not a righteous man on earth who does what is right and never sins.

Ecclesiastes 7:20

Therefore no one will be declared righteous in his sight by observing the law; rather, through the law we become conscious of sin.

Romans 3:20

We all, like sheep, have gone astray, each of us has turned to his own way; and the LORD has laid on him the iniquity of us all.

Isaiah 53:6

You know that Jesus appeared so that he might take away our sins. And in him is no sin. No one who lives in him keeps on sinning. No one who continues to sin has either seen him or known him.

1 John 3:5-6

God's Words of Life on
SIN & TEMPTATION

If we claim to have fellowship with God yet walk in the darkness, we lie and do not live by the truth.

1 John 1:6

If we claim to be without sin, we deceive ourselves and the truth is not in us. If we confess our sins, he is faithful and just and will forgive us our sins and purify us from all unrighteousness. If we claim we have not sinned, we make him out to be a liar and his word has no place in our lives.

1 John 1:8-10

"Although you wash yourself with soda and use an abundance of soap, the stain of your guilt is still before me," declares the Sovereign LORD.

Jeremiah 2:22

He who conceals his sins does not prosper, but whoever confesses and renounces them finds mercy.

Proverbs 28:13

God commands all people everywhere to repent.

Acts 17:30

Submit yourselves, then, to God. Resist the devil, and he will flee from you.

James 4:7

God's Words of Life on
SIN & TEMPTATION

No temptation has seized you except what is common to man. And God is faithful; he will not let you be tempted beyond what you can bear. But when you are tempted, he will also provide a way out so that you can stand up under it.

1 Corinthians 10:13

Be self-controlled and alert. Your enemy the devil prowls around like a roaring lion looking for someone to devour.

1 Peter 5:8

God has delivered us from such a deadly peril, and he will deliver us. On him we have set our hope that he will continue to deliver us.

2 Corinthians 1:10

The Lord will rescue me from every evil attack and will bring me safely to his heavenly kingdom. To him be glory for ever and ever.

2 Timothy 4:18

We know that since Christ was raised from the dead, he cannot die again; death no longer has mastery over him. The death he died, he died to sin once for all; but the life he lives, he lives to God. In the same way, count yourselves dead to sin but alive to God in Christ Jesus.

156

Romans 6:9-11

God's Words of Life on
SIN & TEMPTATION

Jesus said, "Watch and pray so that you will not fall into temptation. The spirit is willing, but the body is weak."

Matthew 26:41

We know that our old self was crucified with Jesus so that the body of sin might be done away with, that we should no longer be slaves to sin—because anyone who has died has been freed from sin.

Romans 6:6-7

Because Christ himself suffered when he was tempted, he is able to help those who are being tempted.

Hebrews 2:18

Jesus said, "I tell you, every sin and blasphemy will be forgiven men, but the blasphemy against the Spirit will not be forgiven."

Matthew 12:31

There is now no condemnation for those who are in Christ Jesus, because through Christ Jesus the law of the Spirit of life set me free from the law of sin and death.

Romans 8:1-2

For the wages of sin is death, but the gift of God is eternal life in Christ Jesus our Lord.

Romans 6:23

God's Words of Life on
SIN & TEMPTATION

"In your anger do not sin:" Do not let the sun go down while you are still angry, and do not give the devil a foothold.

Ephesians 4:26-27

Since we are surrounded by such a great cloud of witnesses, let us throw off everything that hinders and the sin that so easily entangles, and let us run with perseverance the race marked out for us.

Hebrews 12:1

I do not consider myself yet to have taken hold of it. But one thing I do: Forgetting what is behind and straining toward what is ahead, I press on toward the goal to win the prize for which God has called me heavenward in Christ Jesus.

Philippians 3:13-14

Do not be deceived: God cannot be mocked. A man reaps what he sows. The one who sows to please his sinful nature, from that nature will reap destruction; the one who sows to please the Spirit, from the Spirit will reap eternal life.

Galatians 6:7-8

Devotional Thought on
SIN & TEMPTATION

We are never out of the reach of temptation. Both at home and abroad we are liable to meet with allurements to evil; the morning opens with peril, and the shades of evening find us still in jeopardy. Those who think themselves secure are more exposed to danger than any others. The armor-bearer of sin is self-confidence. When I see the King of Israel sluggishly leaving his couch at the close of the day, and falling at once into temptation, let me take warning, and set holy watchfulness to guard the door.

Is it possible that the king had climbed to his housetop for retirement and devotion? If so, what a caution is given us to count no place, however secret, a sanctuary from sin! Since our hearts are so like a tinderbox and sparks so plentiful, we had better use all diligence in all places to prevent a blaze. Satan can climb housetops and enter closets, and even if we could shut out that foul fiend, our own corruptions are enough to work our ruin unless grace prevents. Reader, beware of evening temptations. Do not be secure. The sun is down but sin is up.

Charles H. Spurgeon 159

God's Words of Life on
HIS SOVEREIGNTY

The LORD will reign for ever and ever.

Exodus 15:18

God's Son was given authority, glory and sovereign power; all peoples, nations and men of every language worshiped him. His dominion is an everlasting dominion that will not pass away, and his kingdom is one that will never be destroyed.

Daniel 7:14

God's kingdom will be an everlasting kingdom, and all rulers will worship and obey him.

Daniel 7:27

For the LORD your God is God of gods and LORD of Lords, the great God, mighty and awesome, who shows no partiality and accepts no bribes.

Deuteronomy 10:17

For great is the LORD and most worthy of praise; he is to be feared above all gods.

1 Chronicles 16:25

For the LORD your God is God in heaven above and on the earth below.

Joshua 2:11

God's Words of Life on
HIS SOVEREIGNTY

You alone are the LORD. You made the heavens, even the highest heavens, and all their starry host, the earth and all that is on it, the seas and all that is in them. You give life to everything, and the multitudes of heaven worship you.

Nehemiah 9:6

The earth is the LORD's, and everything in it, the world, and all who live in it.

Psalm 24:1

Let them know that you, whose name is the LORD—that you alone are the Most High over all the earth.

Psalm 83:18

You, O LORD, are the Most High over all the earth; you are exalted far above all gods.

Psalm 97:9

I am the first and I am the last; apart from me there is no God.

Isaiah 44:6

"I am the Alpha and the Omega," says the Lord God, "who is, and who was, and who is to come, the Almighty."

Revelation 1:8

God's Words of Life on
HIS SOVEREIGNTY

I am the LORD, the God of all mankind.

Jeremiah 32:27

God, the blessed and only Ruler, the King of
kings and Lord of Lords.

1 Timothy 6:15

Then the LORD answered Job out of the
storm. "Who is this that darkens my counsel
with words without knowledge? Where were
you when I laid the earth's foundation?
Tell me, if you understand.

Who marked off its dimensions? Who
stretched a measuring line across it? On what
were its footings set, or who laid its corner-
stone—while the morning stars sang together
and all the angels shouted for joy? Who shut
up the sea behind doors when it burst forth
from the womb, when I made the clouds its
garment and wrapped it in thick darkness,
when I fixed limits for it and set its doors
and bars in place, when I said, `This far you
may come and no farther; here is where your
proud waves halt'? Have you ever given
orders to the morning, or shown the dawn
its place, that it might take the earth by the
edges and shake the wicked out of it? The
earth takes shape like clay under a seal; its
features stand out like those of a garment.

Job 38:1-2, 4-14

Devotional Thought on
GOD'S SOVEREIGNTY

Allow me a word with you who murmur. Why should you murmur against the dispensations of your heavenly Father? Can he treat you more harshly than you deserve? Consider what a rebel you once were, but he pardoned you! Surely, if he in his wisdom sees fit to chasten you, you should not complain. Does not that proud, rebellious spirit of yours prove that your heart is not thoroughly sanctified? Those murmuring words are contrary to the holy, submissive nature of God's children. Is not the correction needed? But if you murmur against the chastening, take heed, for it will go hard with murmurers.

But know one thing—"He doth not afflict willingly, nor grieve the children of men" (Lamentations 3:33, KJV). All his corrections are sent in love, to purify you, and to draw you nearer to himself. Surely it must help you bear the chastening if you are able to recognize your Father's hand. For "whom the Lord loveth he chasteneth, and scourgeth every son whom he receiveth. If ye endure chastening, God dealeth with you as with sons" (Hebrews 12:6-7).

Charles H. Spurgeon   163

God's Words of Life on
SPEECH

A man finds joy in giving an apt reply—and how good is a timely word!

Proverbs 15:23

From the fruit of his lips a man is filled with good things as surely as the work of his hands rewards him.

Proverbs 12:14

A perverse man stirs up dissension, and a gossip separates close friends.

Proverbs 16:28

Do not let any unwholesome talk come out of your mouths, but only what is helpful for building others up according to their needs, that it may benefit those who listen.

Ephesians 4:29

Out of the overflow of the heart the mouth speaks.

Matthew 12:34

He who guards his mouth and his tongue keeps himself from calamity.

Proverbs 21:23

Do everything without complaining or arguing.

Philippians 2:14

God's Words of Life on
SPEECH

Let your conversation be always full of grace, seasoned with salt, so that you may know how to answer everyone.

Colossians 4:6

Words from a wise man's mouth are gracious, but a fool is consumed by his own lips.

Ecclesiastes 10:12

He who guards his lips guards his life, but he who speaks rashly will come to ruin.

Proverbs 13:3

If anyone considers himself religious and yet does not keep a tight rein on his tongue, he deceives himself and his religion is worthless.

James 1:26

The tongue has the power of life and death, and those who love it will eat its fruit.

Proverbs 18:21

A word aptly spoken is like apples of gold in settings of silver.

Proverbs 25:11

Let us not love with words or tongue but with actions and in truth.

1 John 3:18

God's Words of Life on
SPEECH

He who loves a pure heart and whose speech is gracious will have the king for his friend.

Proverbs 22:11

Don't let anyone look down on you because you are young, but set an example for the believers in speech, in life, in love, in faith and in purity.

1 Timothy 4:12

Whoever would love life and see good days must keep his tongue from evil and his lips from deceitful speech. He must turn from evil and do good; he must seek peace and pursue it.

1 Peter 3:10-11

The ear tests words as the tongue tastes food.

Job 34:3

LORD, who may dwell in your sanctuary? Who may live on your holy hill? He whose walk is blameless and who does what is righteous, who speaks the truth from his heart and has no slander on his tongue, who does his neighbor no wrong and casts no slur on his fellowman, who despises a vile man but honors those who fear the LORD, who keeps his oath even when it hurts.

Psalm 15:1-4

God's Words of Life on
SPEECH

The mouth of the righteous man utters wisdom, and his tongue speaks what is just. The law of his God is in his heart; his feet do not slip.

Psalm 37: 30-31

The LORD detests lying lips, but he delights in men who are truthful. A prudent man keeps his knowledge to himself, but the heart of fools blurts out folly.

Proverbs 12:22-23

A man who lacks judgment derides his neighbor, but a man of understanding holds his tongue. A gossip betrays a confidence, but a trustworthy man keeps a secret.

Proverbs 11:12-13

Reckless words pierce like a sword, but the tongue of the wise brings healing. Truthful lips endure forever, but a lying tongue lasts only a moment.

Proverbs 12:18-19

He who covers over an offense promotes love, but whoever repeats the matter separates close friends.

Proverbs 17:9

O LORD, my tongue will speak of your righteousness and of your praises all day long.

Psalm 35:28

God's Words of Life on
SPEECH

He who rebukes a man will in the end gain more favor than he who has a flattering tongue.

Proverbs 28:23

Let the word of Christ dwell in you richly as you teach and admonish one another with all wisdom, and as you sing psalms, hymns and spiritual songs with gratitude in your hearts to God. And whatever you do, whether in word or deed, do it all in the name of the Lord Jesus, giving thanks to God the Father through him.

Colossians 3:16-17

With the tongue we praise our Lord and Father, and with it we curse men, who have been made in God's likeness. Out of the same mouth come praise and cursing. My brothers, this should not be.

James 3:9-10

Before a word is on my tongue you know it completely, O LORD. You hem me in- behind and before; you have laid your hand upon me.

Psalm 139:4-5

Devotional Thought on
SPEECH

Lord, speak to me, that I may speak
In living echoes of thy tone;
 As thou hast sought, so let me seek
 Thy erring children lost and lone.
O teach me, Lord, that I may teach
The precious things thou dost impart;
And wing my words, that they may
   reach
The hidden depths of many a heart.
O fill me with thy fullness, Lord,
Until my very heart o'erflow
In kindling thought and glowing word,
Thy love to tell, thy praise to show.
O use me, Lord, use even me,
Just as thou wilt, and when and where;
Until thy blessed face I see,
Thy rest, thy joy, thy glory share.

Frances Ridley Havergal

God's Words of Life on
SPIRITUAL GROWTH

Love the LORD your God with all your heart
and with all your soul and with all your
strength.

Deuteronomy 6:5

Be very careful to keep the commandment
and the law that Moses the servant of the
LORD gave you: to love the LORD your God,
to walk in all his ways, to obey his
commands, to hold fast to him and to serve
him with all your heart and all your soul.

Joshua 22:5

You will keep in perfect peace him whose
mind is steadfast, because he trusts in you.

Isaiah 26:3

For the kingdom of God is not a matter of
eating and drinking, but of righteousness,
peace and joy in the Holy Spirit.

Romans 14:17

Blessed are those who hunger and thirst for
righteousness, for they will be filled.

Matthew 5:6

Do not work for food that spoils, but for
food that endures to eternal life, which the
Son of Man will give you. On him God the
Father has placed his seal of approval.

John 6:27

God's Words of Life on
SPIRITUAL GROWTH

Since, then, you have been raised with Christ, set your hearts on things above, where Christ is seated at the right hand of God. Set your minds on things above, not on earthly things.

Colossians 3:1–2

Only be careful, and watch yourselves closely so that you do not forget the things your eyes have seen or let them slip from your heart as long as you live. Teach them to your children and to their children after them.

Deuteronomy 4:9

This is what the LORD says: "Stand at the crossroads and look; ask for the ancient paths, ask where the good way is, and walk in it, and you will find rest for your souls."

Jeremiah 6:16

Grow in the grace and knowledge of our Lord and Savior Jesus Christ. To him be glory both now and forever! Amen.

2 Peter 3:18

Do your best to present yourself to God as one approved, a workman who does not need to be ashamed and who correctly handles the word of truth.

2 Timothy 2:15

God's Words of Life on
SPIRITUAL GROWTH

He has showed you, O man, what is good. And what does the LORD require of you? To act justly and to love mercy and to walk humbly with your God.

Micah 6:8

This is my prayer: that your love may abound more and more in knowledge and depth of insight, so that you may be able to discern what is best and may be pure and blameless until the day of Christ.

Philippians 1:9–10

Anyone who loves his father or mother more than me is not worthy of me; anyone who loves his son or daughter more than me is not worthy of me; and anyone who does not take his cross and follow me is not worthy of me. Whoever finds his life will lose it, and whoever loses his life for my sake will find it.

Matthew 10:37–39

He who walks righteously and speaks what is right, who rejects gain from extortion and keeps his hand from accepting bribes, who stops his ears against plots of murder and shuts his eyes against contemplating evil— this is the man who will dwell on the heights.

Isaiah 33:15–16

God's Words of Life on
SPIRITUAL GROWTH

Being confident of this, that he who began a good work in you will carry it on to completion until the day of Christ Jesus.

Philippians 1:6

"He follows my decrees and faithfully keeps my laws. That man is righteous; he will surely live," declares the Sovereign LORD.

Ezekiel 18:9

Jesus replied, "If anyone loves me, he will obey my teaching. My Father will love him, and we will come to him and make our home with him.

John 14:23

Remain in me, and I will remain in you. No branch can bear fruit by itself; it must remain in the vine. Neither can you bear fruit unless you remain in me. I am the vine; you are the branches. If a man remains in me and I in him, he will bear much fruit; apart from me you can do nothing.

John 15:4–5

One thing I do: Forgetting what is behind and straining toward what is ahead, I press on toward the goal to win the prize for which God has called me heavenward in Christ Jesus.

Philippians 3:13–14

God's Words of Life on
SPIRITUAL GROWTH

I pray that out of his glorious riches he may
strengthen you with power through his Spirit
in your inner being, so that Christ may dwell
in your hearts through faith. And I pray that
you, being rooted and established in love,
may have power, together with all the saints,
to grasp how wide and long and high and
deep is the love of Christ, and to know this
love that surpasses knowledge—that you
may be filled to the measure of all the fullness of God.

Ephesians 3:16-19

Put on the full armor of God, so that when
the day of evil comes, you may be able to
stand your ground, and after you have done
everything, to stand. Stand firm then, with
the belt of truth buckled around your waist,
with the breastplate of righteousness in
place, and with your feet fitted with the
readiness that comes from the gospel of
peace. In addition to all this, take up the
shield of faith, with which you can extin-
guish all the flaming arrows of the evil one.
Take the helmet of salvation and the sword
of the Spirit, which is the word of God.

Ephesians 6:13-17

Devotional Thought on
SPIRITUAL GROWTH

As soon as you begin to live the life of faith in God, fascinating and physically gratifying possibilities will open up before you. These things are yours by right, but if you are living the life of faith you will exercise your right to waive your rights, and let God make your choice for you.

Whenever our right becomes the guiding factor of our lives, it dulls our spiritual insight. The greatest enemy of the life of faith in God is not sin, but good choices which are not quite good enough.

Many of us do not continue to grow spiritually because we prefer to choose on the basis of our rights, instead of relying on God to make the choice for us. We have to learn to walk according to the standard which has its eyes focused on God. And God says to us, as he did to Abram, "… walk before me …" (Genesis 17:1).

Oswald Chambers

God's Words of Life on
STRENGTH

The LORD gives strength to his people; the LORD blesses his people with peace.

Psalm 29:11

Do not fear, for I am with you; do not be dismayed, for I am your God. I will strengthen you and help you; I will uphold you with my righteous right hand.

Isaiah 41:10

He said to me, "My grace is sufficient for you, for my power is made perfect in weakness." Therefore I will boast all the more gladly about my weaknesses, so that Christ's power may rest on me. That is why, for Christ's sake, I delight in weaknesses, in insults, in hardships, in persecutions, in difficulties. For when I am weak, then I am strong.

2 Corinthians 12:9–10

I can do everything through Christ who gives me strength.

Philippians 4:13

I pray that out of his glorious riches he may strengthen you with power through his Spirit in your inner being, so that Christ may dwell in your hearts through faith.

Ephesians 3:16–17

God's Words of Life on
STRENGTH

The LORD is the strength of his people, a fortress of salvation for his anointed one.

Psalm 28:8

In the LORD alone are righteousness and strength.

Isaiah 45:24

Those who hope in the LORD will renew their strength. They will soar on wings like eagles; they will run and not grow weary, they will walk and not be faint.

Isaiah 40:31

"I will strengthen them in the LORD and in his name they will walk," declares the LORD.

Zechariah 10:12

Wealth and honor come from you, O LORD; you are the ruler of all things. In your hands are strength and power to exalt and give strength to all.

1 Chronicles 29:12

Since we are surrounded by such a great cloud of witnesses, let us throw off everything that hinders and the sin that so easily entangles, and let us run with perseverance the race marked out for us.

Hebrews 12:1

God's Words of Life on
STRENGTH

Strengthen me according to your word, O LORD.

Psalm 119:28

Do your best to present yourself to God as one approved, a workman who does not need to be ashamed and who correctly handles the word of truth.

2 Timothy 2:15

The Lord stood at my side and gave me strength, so that through me the message might be fully proclaimed. The Lord will rescue me from every evil attack and will bring me safely to his heavenly kingdom. To him be glory for ever and ever. Amen.

2 Timothy 4:17-18

David found strength in the LORD his God.

1 Samuel 30:4

God gives strength to the weary and increases the power of the weak.

Isaiah 40:29

Devotional Thought on
STRENGTH

H e was crucified through weakness" (2 Corinthians 13:4). Jesus Christ represents God limiting his own power for one purpose: he died for the weak, for the ungodly, for sinners, and for no one else. "I have not come to call the righteous, but sinners to repentance" (Luke 5:32).

The "strong man" idea is the one that appeals to men, the strong man physically, morally, strong in every way; the kingdoms of men are to be founded on strong men and the weakest are to go to the wall. History proves, however, that it is the strongest that go to the wall, not the weakest.

In all trade and commerce there is oppression, and we try to justify it by saying that the weakest must go to the wall. But is that so? Where are the mighty civilizations of other days? Where are the prehistoric animals, those colossal powerful creatures? It is they that have gone to the wall. The great blunder in all kingdoms among men is that we will demand strong men, consequently each kingdom in its turn goes to the wall because no chain is stronger than its weakest link.

Oswald Chambers

God's Words of Life on
SURRENDER

Submit to one another out of reverence for Christ.

Ephesians 5:21

I desire to do your will, O my God; your law is within my heart.

Psalm 40:8

Praise the LORD. Blessed is the man who fears the LORD, who finds great delight in his commands.

Psalm 112:1

I delight in your commands, O LORD, because I love them. I lift up my hands to your commands, which I love, and I meditate on your decrees.

Psalm 119:47–48

Jesus went away a second time and prayed, "My Father, if it is not possible for this cup to be taken away unless I drink it, may your will be done."

Matthew 26:42

Jesus replied, "Not everyone who says to me, "Lord, Lord," will enter the kingdom of heaven, but only he who does the will of my Father who is in heaven."

Matthew 7:21

God's Words of Life on
SURRENDER

Being found in appearance as a man, he humbled himself and became obedient to death—even death on a cross! Therefore God exalted him to the highest place and gave him the name that is above every name, that at the name of Jesus every knee should bow, in heaven and on earth and under the earth, and every tongue confess that Jesus Christ is Lord, to the glory of God the Father.

Philippians 2:8–11

Let us fix our eyes on Jesus, the author and perfecter of our faith, who for the joy set before him endured the cross, scorning its shame, and sat down at the right hand of the throne of God. Consider him who endured such opposition from sinful men, so that you will not grow weary and lose heart.

Hebrews 12:2–3

Jesus replied, "I seek not to please myself but him who sent me."

John 5:30

During the days of Jesus' life on earth, he offered up prayers and petitions with loud cries and tears to the one who could save him from death, and he was heard because of his reverent submission. Although he was a son, he learned obedience from what he suffered.

Hebrews 5:7–8

God's Words of Life on
SURRENDER

I will never forget your precepts, O LORD, for by them you have preserved my life. Save me, for I am yours.

Psalm 119:93–94

If you confess with your mouth, "Jesus is Lord," and believe in your heart that God raised him from the dead, you will be saved.

Romans 10:9

Offer your bodies as living sacrifices, holy and pleasing to God—this is your spiritual act of worship. Do not conform any longer to the pattern of this world, but be transformed by the renewing of your mind. Then you will be able to test and approve what God's will is—his good, pleasing and perfect will.

Romans 12:1–2

If we live, we live to the Lord; and if we die, we die to the Lord. So, whether we live or die, we belong to the Lord.

Romans 14:8

Does the LORD delight in burnt offerings and sacrifices as much as in obeying the voice of the LORD? To obey is better than sacrifice, and to heed is better than the fat of rams.

1 Samuel 15:22

You were bought at a price. Therefore honor God with your body.

1 Corinthians 6:20

Submit yourselves for the Lord's sake to every authority instituted among men: whether to the king, as the supreme authority, or to governors, who are sent by him to punish those who do wrong and to commend those who do right. For it is God's will that by doing good you should silence the ignorant talk of foolish men. Live as free men, but do not use your freedom as a cover-up for evil; live as servants of God.

1 Peter 2:13–16

Jesus replied, "Whoever has my commands and obeys them, he is the one who loves me. He who loves me will be loved by my Father, and I too will love him and show myself to him."

John 14:21

May the God who gives endurance and encouragement give you a spirit of unity among yourselves as you follow Christ Jesus, so that with one heart and mouth you may glorify the God and Father of our Lord Jesus Christ.

Romans 15:5-6

God's Words of Life on
SURRENDER

Godliness with contentment is great gain.

1 Timothy 6:6

Pursue righteousness, godliness, faith, love, endurance and gentleness. Fight the good fight of the faith. Take hold of the eternal life to which you were called when you made your good confession in the presence of many witnesses.

1 Timothy 6:11-12

All Scripture is God-breathed and is useful for teaching, rebuking, correcting and training in righteousness, so that the man of God may be thoroughly equipped for every good work.

2 Timothy 3:16-17

Continue to work out your salvation with fear and trembling, for it is God who works in you to will and to act according to his good purpose.

Philippians 2:12-13

So then, just as you received Christ Jesus as Lord, continue to live in him, rooted and built up in him, strengthened in the faith as you were taught, and overflowing with thankfulness.

Colossians 2:6-7

Devotional Thought on
SURRENDER

Dear Souls! How little they know that the abiding in Christ is just meant for the weak, and so beautifully suited to their feebleness. It is not the doing of some great thing, and does not demand that we first lead a very holy and devoted life. No, it is simply weakness entrusting itself to a Mighty One to be kept—the unfaithful one casting self on One who is altogether trustworthy and true. Abiding in him is not a work that we have to do as the condition for enjoying his salvation, but a consenting to let him do all for us, and in us, and through us. It is a work he does for us— the fruit and the power of his redeeming love. Our part is simply to yield, to trust, and to wait for what he has engaged to perform.

Andrew Murray

God's Words of Life on
THANKFULNESS

Know that the LORD is God. It is he who made us, and we are his; we are his people, the sheep of his pasture. Enter his gates with thanksgiving and his courts with praise; give thanks to him and praise his name.

Psalm 100:3–4

Let us continually offer to God a sacrifice of praise—the fruit of lips that confess his name.

Hebrews 13:15

I thank my God every time I remember you.

Philippians 1:3

So then, just as you received Christ Jesus as Lord, continue to live in him, rooted and built up in him, strengthened in the faith as you were taught, and overflowing with thankfulness.

Colossians 2:6–7

Let the word of Christ dwell in you richly as you teach and admonish one another with all wisdom, and as you sing psalms, hymns and spiritual songs with gratitude in your hearts to God. Whatever you do, whether in word or deed, do it all in the name of the Lord Jesus, giving thanks to God the Father through him.

Colossians 3:16–17

God's Words of Life on
THANKFULNESS

Speak to one another with psalms, hymns and spiritual songs. Sing and make music in your heart to the Lord, always giving thanks to God the Father for everything, in the name of our Lord Jesus Christ.

Ephesians 5:19–20

Give thanks in all circumstances, for this is God's will for you in Christ Jesus.

1 Thessalonians 5:18

Do not be anxious about anything, but in everything, by prayer and petition, with thanksgiving, present your requests to God.

Philippians 4:6

Since we are receiving a kingdom that cannot be shaken, let us be thankful, and so worship God acceptably with reverence and awe.

Hebrews 12:28

Give thanks to the LORD, call on his name; make known among the nations what he has done.

1 Chronicles 16:8

I will give thanks to the LORD because of his righteousness and will sing praise to the name of the LORD Most High.

Psalm 7:17

God's Words of Life on
THANKFULNESS

The LORD is my strength and my shield; my heart trusts in him, and I am helped. My heart leaps for joy and I will give thanks to him in song.

Psalm 28:7

You turned my wailing into dancing; you removed my sackcloth and clothed me with joy, that my heart may sing to you and not be silent. O LORD, my God, I will give you thanks forever.

Psalm 30:11–12

Give thanks to the LORD, for he is good; his love endures forever. Let the redeemed of the LORD say this.

Psalm 107:1–2

Give thanks to the LORD, for he is good. His love endures forever. Give thanks to the God of gods. His love endures forever. Give thanks to the LORD of Lords: His love endures forever.

Psalm 136:1–3

Wealth and honor come from you; you are the ruler of all things. In your hands are strength and power to exalt and give strength to all. Now, our God, we give you thanks, and praise your glorious name.

1 Chronicles 29:12–13

God's Words of Life on
THANKFULNESS

Thanks be to God! He gives us the victory through our Lord Jesus Christ.

1 Corinthians 15:57

You are my God, and I will give you thanks; you are my God, and I will exalt you. Give thanks to the LORD, for he is good; his love endures forever.

Psalm 118:28–29

I have not stopped giving thanks for you, remembering you in my prayers.

Ephesians 1:16

Give thanks to the LORD for his unfailing love and his wonderful deeds for men, for he satisfies the thirsty and fills the hungry with good things.

Psalm 107:8–9

I will give you thanks, O LORD, for you answered me; you have become my salvation.

Psalm 118:21

We give thanks to you, O God, we give thanks, for your Name is near; men tell of your wonderful deeds.

Psalm 75:1

Praise the LORD. Give thanks to the LORD, for he is good; his love endures forever.

Psalm 106:1

God's Words of Life on
THANKFULNESS

Thanks be to God, who always leads us in triumphal procession in Christ and through us spreads everywhere the fragrance of the knowledge of him. For we are to God the aroma of Christ among those who are being saved and those who are perishing.

2 Corinthians 2:14-15

Give thanks to the LORD, for he is good; his love endures forever.

1 Chronicles 16:34

And whatever you do, whether in word or deed, do it all in the name of the Lord Jesus, giving thanks to God the Father through him.

Colossians 3:17

Praise and glory and wisdom and thanks and honor and power and strength be to our God for ever and ever. Amen!

Revelation 7:12

We give thanks to you, Lord God Almighty, the One who is and who was, because you have taken your great power and have begun to reign.

Revelation 11:17

Devotional Thought on
THANKFULNESS

It is easy to sing when we can read the notes by daylight; but he is skillful who sings when there is not a ray of light to read by, who sings from his heart. No man can make a song in the night of himself; he may attempt it, but he will find that a song in the night must be divinely inspired. Let all things go well, I can weave songs, fashioning them wherever I go out of the flowers that grow on my path; but put me in a desert, where no green thing grows, and wherewith shall I frame a hymn of praise to God?

No, it is not in man's power to sing when all is adverse ... Since our Maker gives *songs in the night,* let us wait on him for the music ... Let us not remain songless because affliction is upon us, but tune our lips to the melody of thanksgiving.

Charles H. Spurgeon

God's Words of Life on
TRUST

Those who know your name will trust in you, for you, LORD, have never forsaken those who seek you.

Psalm 9:10

Blessed is the man who trusts in the LORD, whose confidence is in him. He will be like a tree planted by the water that sends out its roots by the stream. It does not fear when heat comes; its leaves are always green. It has no worries in a year of drought and never fails to bear fruit.

Jeremiah 17:7–8

Abraham did not waver through unbelief regarding the promise of God, but was strengthened in his faith and gave glory to God, being fully persuaded that God had power to do what he had promised.

Romans 4:20–21

Taste and see that the LORD is good; blessed is the man who takes refuge in him.

Psalm 34:8

You will keep in perfect peace him whose mind is steadfast, because he trusts in you. Trust in the LORD forever, for the LORD, the LORD, is the Rock eternal.

Isaiah 26:3–4

God's Words of Life on
TRUST

O LORD Almighty, blessed is the man who trusts in you.

Psalm 84:12

Those who trust in the LORD are like Mount Zion, which cannot be shaken but endures forever.

Psalm 125:1

Whoever gives heed to instruction prospers, and blessed is he who trusts in the LORD.

Proverbs 16:20

Many are the woes of the wicked, but the LORD's unfailing love surrounds the man who trusts in him.

Psalm 32:10

Trust in the LORD and do good; dwell in the land and enjoy safe pasture.

Psalm 37:3

Blessed is the man who makes the LORD his trust, who does not look to the proud, to those who turn aside to false gods.

Psalm 40:4

Trust in the LORD with all your heart and lean not on your own understanding; in all your ways acknowledge him, and he will make your paths straight.

Proverbs 3:5-6

God's Words of Life on
TRUST

A greedy man stirs up dissension, but he who trusts in the LORD will prosper.

Proverbs 28:25

As the Scripture says, "Anyone who trusts in God will never be put to shame."

Romans 10:11

Be strong and take heart, all you who hope in the LORD.

Psalm 31:24

"When you pass through the waters, I will be with you; and when you pass through the rivers, they will not sweep over you. When you walk through the fire, you will not be burned; the flames will not set you ablaze," says the LORD.

Isaiah 43:2

Offer right sacrifices and trust in the LORD.

Psalm 4:5

God is my salvation; I will trust and not be afraid. The LORD, the LORD, is my strength and my song.

Isaiah 12:2

Jesus replied, "Do not let your hearts be troubled. Trust in God; trust also in me."

John 14:1

Devotional Thought on
TRUST

There are secrets of providence which God's dear children may learn. His dealings with them often seem, to the outward eye, dark and terrible. Faith looks deeper and says, "This is God's secret. You look only on the outside; I can look deeper and see the hidden meaning."

Sometimes diamonds are done up in rough packages, so that their value cannot be seen. When the tabernacle was built in the wilderness there was nothing rich in its outside appearance. The costly things were all within, and its outward covering of rough badger skin gave no hint of the valuable things which it contained.

God may send you, dear friends, some costly packages. Do not worry if they are done up in rough wrapping. You may be sure there are treasures of love, and kindness, and wisdom hidden within. If we take what he sends, *and trust him* for the goodness in it, even in the dark, we shall learn the meaning of the secrets of providence.

A.B. Simpson

God's Words of Life on
VALUES

Jesus said, "So in everything, do to others what you would have them do to you, for this sums up the Law and the Prophets."

Matthew 7:12

Jesus replied: "'Love the Lord your God with all your heart and with all your soul and with all your mind.' This is the first and greatest commandment. And the second is like it: 'Love your neighbor as yourself.' All the Law and the Prophets hang on these two commandments."

Matthew 22:37–40

The things that come out of the mouth come from the heart.

Matthew 15:18

LORD, who may dwell in your sanctuary? Who may live on your holy hill? He whose walk is blameless and who does what is righteous, who speaks the truth from his heart and has no slander on his tongue, who does his neighbor no wrong and casts no slur on his fellowman, who despises a vile man but honors those who fear the LORD, who keeps his oath even when it hurts, who lends his money without usury and does not accept a bribe against the innocent. He who does these things will never be shaken.

Psalm 15:1–5

God's Words of Life on
VALUES

The fruit of the Spirit is love, joy, peace, patience, kindness, goodness, faithfulness, gentleness and self-control. Against such things there is no law.

Galatians 5:22–23

He has showed you, O man, what is good. And what does the LORD require of you? To act justly and to love mercy and to walk humbly with your God.

Micah 6:8

Be careful that you do not forget the LORD your God, failing to observe his commands, his laws and his decrees.

Deuteronomy 8:11

Keep falsehood and lies far from me; give me neither poverty nor riches, but give me only my daily bread. Otherwise, I may have too much and disown you and say, "Who is the LORD?" Or I may become poor and steal, and so dishonor the name of my God.

Proverbs 30:8–9

Who may ascend the hill of the LORD? Who may stand in his holy place? He who has clean hands and a pure heart, who does not lift up his soul to an idol or swear by what is false.

Psalm 24:3–4

God's Words of Life on
VALUES

This is what the LORD says: "Stand at the crossroads and look; ask for the ancient paths, ask where the good way is, and walk in it, and you will find rest for your souls."

Jeremiah 6:16

Better a poor man whose walk is blameless than a rich man whose ways are perverse.

Proverbs 28:6

The noble man makes noble plans, and by noble deeds he stands.

Isaiah 32:8

Blessed is the man who does not walk in the counsel of the wicked or stand in the way of sinners or sit in the seat of mockers. But his delight is in the law of the LORD, and on his law he meditates day and night. He is like a tree planted by streams of water, which yields its fruit in season and whose leaf does not wither. Whatever he does prospers.

Psalm 1:1–3

Love the LORD your God with all your heart and with all your soul and with all your strength.

Deuteronomy 6:5

Devotional Thought on
VALUES

W alk through a museum and you will
see all the orders of animals standing
in their various places and exhibiting themselves with the utmost possible propriety.
Every creature, whether bird, beast or fish
remains in the particular glass case allotted
to it. But we know that these are not the
creatures, but only the outward semblances
of them. Yet in what do they differ?
Certainly in nothing which you could
readily see, for the well-stuffed animal is
precisely like what the living animal would
have been. That eye of glass even appears to
have more brightness in it than the natural
eye of the creature itself. But there is a secret
inward something lacking, which, when it
has once departed, you cannot restore. So in
the church of Christ, many professing
believers are not living believers, but stuffed
Christians. They possess all the externals of
religion, and every outward morality that
you could desire. They behave with great
propriety, they keep their places, and there
is no outward difference between them and
the true believer, except upon the vital
point, the life which no power on earth can
possibly confer.

Charles H. Spurgeon   199

God's Words of Life on
WEAKNESS

Do not be afraid or discouraged, for the LORD God, my God, is with you. He will not fail you or forsake you.

1 Chronicles 28:20

If we are faithless, he [Jesus] will remain faithful, for he cannot disown himself.

2 Timothy 2:13

For we do not have a high priest who is unable to sympathize with our weaknesses, but we have one who has been tempted in every way, just as we are—yet was without sin. Let us then approach the throne of grace with confidence, so that we may receive mercy and find grace to help us in our time of need.

Hebrews 4:15–16

He said to me, "My grace is sufficient for you, for my power is made perfect in weakness." Therefore I will boast all the more gladly about my weaknesses, so that Christ's power may rest on me.

2 Corinthians 12:9

Though I walk in the midst of trouble, you, O LORD, preserve my life; you stretch out your hand against the anger of my foes, with your right hand you save me.

Psalm 138:7

God's Words of Life on
WEAKNESS

We know that in all things God works for the good of those who love him, who have been called according to his purpose.

Romans 8:28

I lift up my eyes to the hills—where does my help come from? My help comes from the LORD, the Maker of heaven and earth.

Psalm 121:1–2

Jesus replied, "Watch and pray so that you will not fall into temptation. The spirit is willing, but the body is weak."

Matthew 26:41

Jesus was crucified in weakness, yet he lives by God's power. Likewise, we are weak in him, yet by God's power we will live with him.

2 Corinthians 13:4

The Spirit helps us in our weakness. We do not know what we ought to pray for, but the Spirit himself intercedes for us with groans that words cannot express.

Romans 8:26

We who are strong ought to bear with the failings of the weak and not to please ourselves.

Romans 15:1

God's Words of Life on
WEAKNESS

The foolishness of God is wiser than man's wisdom, and the weakness of God is stronger than man's strength.

1 Corinthians 1:25

God chose the foolish things of the world to shame the wise; God chose the weak things of the world to shame the strong. He chose the lowly things of this world and the despised things—and the things that are not—to nullify the things that are, so that no one may boast before him.

1 Corinthians 1:27–29

"Not by might nor by power, but by my Spirit," says the LORD Almighty.

Zechariah 4:6

You are weak in your natural selves. Just as you used to offer the parts of your body in slavery to impurity and to ever-increasing wickedness, so now offer them in slavery to righteousness leading to holiness.

Romans 6:19

Devotional Thought on
WEAKNESS

I distinctly remember the day when I left home to face life, amid its crowded ways, for myself. My father, whose philosophy was certainly that of the Hebrew wisdom, gave me [Proverbs 3:5-6] as providing a complete guide to life. Looking back over the intervening years I know he was right. In them there has been much of failure, many turnings aside from the straight highway, many devious and sorrowful wanderings from the true paths of life. All such failure, such turnings aside, such wanderings, have resulted from leaning to one's own understanding. The measure in which I have trusted Jehovah, and acknowledged him, has been the measure of walking in the paths of real life. Doubt of God, pride of intellect, and independence in volition, these are the things which blight and blast. Paths chosen for us by God all lead onward and upward, even when they seem to us to turn about in inextricable confusion, and to move downward to the valleys of humiliation and suffering. He is the All-Wise, and to him, wisdom is the way by which Love gains his victory.

G. Campbell Morgan

God's Words of Life on
WISDOM

Your commands, O LORD, make me wiser, for they are ever with me.

Psalm 119:98

And he said to man, "The fear of the Lord—that is wisdom, and to shun evil is understanding."

Job 28:28

"I will instruct you and teach you in the way you should go; I will counsel you and watch over you," says the LORD.

Psalm 32:8

Jesus replied, "Therefore everyone who hears these words of mine and puts them into practice is like a wise man who built his house on the rock. The rain came down, the streams rose, and the winds blew and beat against that house; yet it did not fall, because it had its foundation on the rock."

Matthew 7:24–25

Get wisdom, get understanding; do not forget my words or swerve from them. Do not forsake wisdom, and she will protect you; love her, and she will watch over you. Wisdom is supreme; therefore get wisdom. Though it cost all you have, get understanding.

Proverbs 4:5–7

God's Words of Life on
WISDOM

"I guide you in the way of wisdom and lead you along straight paths. When you walk, your steps will not be hampered; when you run, you will not stumble," declares the LORD.

Proverbs 4:11–12

Trust in the LORD with all your heart and lean not on your own understanding; in all your ways acknowledge him, and he will make your paths straight. Do not be wise in your own eyes.

Proverbs 3:5–7

Do you not know? Have you not heard? The LORD is the everlasting God, the Creator of the ends of the earth. He will not grow tired or weary, and his understanding no one can fathom.

Isaiah 40:28

The wisdom that comes from heaven is first of all pure; then peace-loving, considerate, submissive, full of mercy and good fruit, impartial and sincere.

James 3:17

"My son, pay attention to my wisdom, listen well to my words of insight, that you may maintain discretion and your lips may preserve knowledge," declares the LORD.

Proverbs 5:1–2

God's Words of Life on
WISDOM

My son, if you accept my words and store up my commands within you, turning your ear to wisdom and applying your heart to understanding, and if you call out for insight and cry aloud for understanding, and if you look for it as for silver and search for it as for hidden treasure, then you will understand the fear of the LORD and find the knowledge of God. For the LORD gives wisdom, and from his mouth come knowledge and understanding.

Proverbs 2:1–6

Where then does wisdom come from? Where does understanding dwell? It is hidden from the eyes of every living thing, concealed even from the birds of the air. God understands the way to it and he alone knows where it dwells.

Job 28:20–21,23

For the foolishness of God is wiser than man's wisdom, and the weakness of God is stronger than man's strength.

1 Corinthians 1:25

If any of you lacks wisdom, he should ask God, who gives generously to all without finding fault, and it will be given to him.

James 1:5

Devotional Thought on
WISDOM

Wherein does true wisdom consist? Were I to ask some of you, perhaps you would say, true wisdom consisted in adding house to house, and field to field, and calling lands after their own names: but this cannot be true wisdom; for riches often take to themselves wings, and fly away.

Perhaps you place wisdom in the knowledge of books: but learned men are not always wise. To keep you therefore no longer in suspense, I will send you to a heathen to learn what true wisdom is: "Know thyself," was a saying of one of the wise men of Greece; this is certainly true wisdom, and this is that wisdom spoken of in [1 Corinthians 1:30], and which Jesus Christ is made to all elect sinners—they are made to know themselves, so as not to think more highly of themselves than they ought to think. Before, they were darkness; now, they are light in the Lord. They now see that all their righteousnesses are but as filthy rags. That there is no name given under heaven, whereby they can be saved, but that of Jesus Christ, thus Christ is made to them wisdom.

George Whitefield   207

Other titles to enjoy in the
God's Words of Life Series include:

*God's Words of Life from the
Men's Devotional Bible*

*God's Words of Life from the
Women's Devotional Bible 2*

*God's Words of Life from the
New Student Bible*

Zondervan*Gifts*

We have a gift for inspiration™